PAPER QUILTS

"Patchwork? Ah, no! It was memory, imagination, history, biography, joy, sorrow, philosophy, religion, romance, realism, life, love, and death; and overall, like a halo, the love of the artist for (her) work and the soul's longing for earthly immortality."
—*Eliza Calvert Hall 1907*

Published in the United States by Potter Craft,
an imprint of the Crown Publishing Group,
a division of Random House, Inc., New York

www.crownpublishing.com

www.pottercraft.com

POTTER CRAFT and colophon, and POTTER and colophon
are registered trademarks of Random House, Inc.

Library of Congress Cataloging-in-Publication Data

Foose, Sandra Lounsbury,

Paper quilts: turn traditional quilt motifs into contemporary cards and crafts/
Sandra Lounsbury Foose.—1st ed.

p.cm

Includes Index.

ISBN: 978-0-307-34147-1 (pbk. : alk. paper)

1. Greeting cards. 2. Quilting. I. Title

Printed in China

Cover and graphic design by LaTricia Watford

1 3 5 7 9 10 8 6 4 2

First Edition

PAPER QUILTS

Turn Traditional Quilt Motifs into Contemporary Cards and Crafts

POTTER
CRAFT

Sandra Lounsbury Foose

ACKNOWLEDGMENTS

Although I have not had the pleasure of meeting either Barbara Brackman or Jonathan Holstein, I am deeply grateful to each of them for the work they have done to inspire *Paper Quilts*.

In the late 1960s, author, quilt collector, and historian Jonathan Holstein recognized and celebrated the visual connection between intellectual twentieth-century abstract art and ingenious nineteenth-century American quilts. He proceeded to imagine, propose, and create the 1970 landmark exhibit, "Abstract Design in American Quilts" for the Whitney Museum of Art in New York. That event was a turning point, creating an international appreciation for American quilts and causing the humble bed covering to be viewed as artwork and social document.

Author and quilt historian Barbara Brackman compiled the *Encyclopedia of Pieced Quilt Patterns* and stuffed it with drawings, names, and sources for the more than 4,000 American quilt patterns that were published between 1830 and 1970. Her amazing "idea factory" book, published by the American Quilter's Society in 1993, was the primary resource and inspiration for *Paper Quilts*.

Thanks are also due to my very good-natured editor, Mona Michael, who picked up the pieces, put them all together, and made *Paper Quilts*.

DEDICATION

With great appreciation and admiration for their resourcefulness, creativity, skill, and wit, I dedicate this book to the memory of The Quiltmakers, especially those who created the fabric of my life—Bertha, Mary Catherine, Annie, Maggie, and Ruth.

—Sandra Lounsbury Foose 2007

CONTENTS

INTRODUCTION

Stars and Stripes, Yankee Pride, New Frontier, Indian Trails, Wandering Foot, Steps to Glory, Forbidden Fruit, Devil's Claws, Blazing Star, Harvest Moon, Storm at Sea, Streaks O'Lightning, Falling Timber, Wagon Wheels, Wild Goose Chase, Shoo Fly, Broken Dishes, Card Tricks, Bachelor's Puzzle, Love Knot, Wedding Ring, Baby Blocks, Jack in the Box, Razzle Dazzle, Zig Zag!

For hundreds of years, the fanciful names of American quilt patterns have reflected the regional folklore, everyday life, geographic location, religious persuasion, and the wit and whimsy of the quiltmaker. Today just the sound of these folkloric names awakens the creative spirit and inspires wonderful images in the mind's eye. In a world of ever-changing styles and remarkable technological advances, the appeal of patchwork quilts has endured for centuries. Fascinating us with their complexity and geometric precision, patchwork patterns can also be as basic and as playful as a set of building blocks.

Offering a new look at an old tradition, *Paper Quilts* will teach you how to cut corners and create paper portraits of classic American patchwork. Although nothing can ever take the place of a fine old fabric quilt, *Paper Quilts* will enable you to "cut-and-piece" intricate patchwork in a matter of minutes–no pins, no needles, no stitches at all! Creating this collection of miniature quilt motifs requires only a craft knife, a straightedge, an assortment of papers, and a little glue. Using basic cut, fold, and paste techniques, it's easy to transform even little bits and pieces of scrap paper into whimsical notecards and other petite patchwork projects.

Through the years, handmade quilts have been stitched to tell stories, comfort people, brighten homes, honor achievements, and celebrate joyful occasions of the heart. Handmade paper quilt cards can acknowledge or celebrate the same occasions: engagements, weddings, babies, birthdays, housewarmings, thank yous, hellos, and goodbyes.

From one generation to the next and one region to another, women have passed along the American quilting tradition, mixing and adapting patterns to their own use and sharing them with others who did the same. Drawing on this inspiration from the past, start making some paper quilts to delight the eye, warm the heart, and continue the creative process of quilt evolution!

Four-Pointed Star Ornaments (page 58)

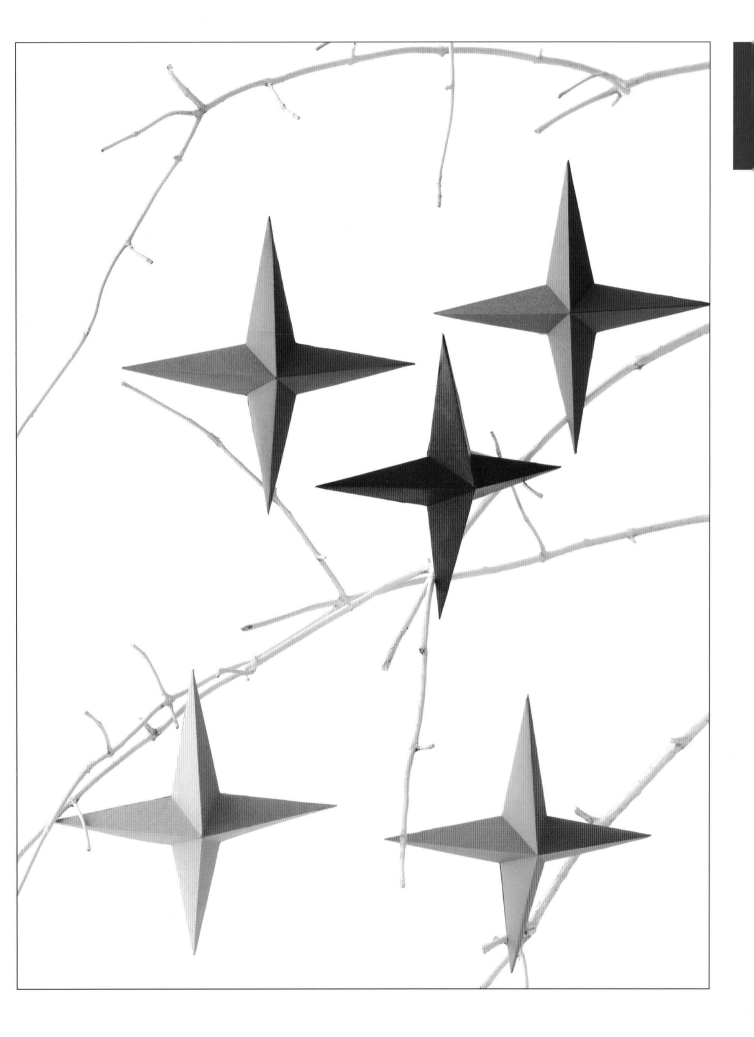

1

BUILDING BLOCKS

Find a pencil and grab your scissors, Paper Quilt Class is about to begin. Before starting any new constructions, read through this chapter for a basic foundation of information that will come in handy as you complete the cards. Learn about rules and tools—placing and erasing. It's all right here, so read on.

Economy Patch Projects (page 26)

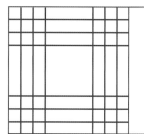

A PAPER PRIMER

Look for paper treasures everywhere! Start with paper stores and card shops and move on to art and craft centers and mail order catalogs. Then check out discount chains, office suppliers, and party stores. When you travel, especially internationally, look for papers to bring home and add to your collection. Read Collecting Scraps below to learn about finding freebies. Set up your own little paper pantry so you will always have a delectable assortment of ingredients close at hand. Here are some of the many types of paper you will encounter in this book and in your own search.

Art Paper

These high-quality, heavy-weight papers are made by Canson, Crescent, Canford, Strathmore, Fabriano, and other manufacturers. Richly hued, subtly textured art papers inspire the heart, eye, and hand. Unlike construction paper, which fades easily and splits when scored and folded, art paper holds its color and has good strength and memory.

Craft stores frequently display art paper in the drawing supply aisle. You can usually find at least one of the brands listed above in any fine art store, and some mail order companies will even send you a swatch book of papers.

Without spending a single penny, you can create a fabulous paper palette from scraps, leftovers, and throwaways.

Text Paper

Available in white and a rainbow of wonderful colors, this ordinary, inexpensive, stationery-weight paper usually measures 8½ by 11 inches (21.6 by 27.9cm). Paper stores and copy shops often carry matching envelopes.

Duplex Paper

Also called duet paper, duplex paper is a light- to medium-weight multipurpose paper with a different color, sometimes just white, on each side of a single sheet. To make your own duplex paper, see Preparing Paper paragraph on page 15.

Japanese Papers

Of the many Japanese papers available, only origami and chiyogami papers were used in this book. Traditional light-weight origami paper is easy to find in packages of brightly colored squares, but it is also available in metallic foil, double-sided, iridescent, luminescent, opalescent, and Japanese folk-art print assortments. Brilliantly colored chiyogami paper is silkscreened with exquisite repeating patterns. It is medium-weight, fade-resistant, and strong yet soft to the touch.

Kraft Paper

Humble but handsome and easy to salvage, kraft paper is most often used for bagging groceries and wrapping parcels because of its strength and low cost. Now and then you may encounter kraft paper enhanced with a printed design or brushed with a metallic wash, and the look is surprisingly elegant.

Scrapbooking Papers

These beautifully colored, patterned, and embossed papers are sold singly, in booklets, or in packs, and they are absolutely irresistible!

Wallpaper

Uncoated sheets of upscale wallpaper cut from an old sample book were used to make several of the projects. Wallpaper samples also make wonderful place mats, shelf liners, book covers, photomats, and gift wraps.

Collecting Scraps

Without spending a single penny, you can create a fabulous paper palette from scraps, leftovers, and throwaways. Gift-giving occasions yield wrappings and boxes, as well as the colorful paper of greeting cards, envelopes, and their linings. Packaging materials worth salvaging could be lurking just inside the shopping bags and other merchandise you regularly carry home. Even the mailbox holds potential treasures in the form of advertisements, invitations, annual reports, catalogs, and promotional mailings. The inside surfaces of white business envelopes are sometimes printed with small, dense patterns to increase the opacity, so save those too, if they look interesting.

Check for unusual colors, patterns, and textures on folders, shopping bags, stationery, calendars, playing cards, newspapers, maps, the covers of old notebooks, paint chip cards, manufacturers' tags hanging on clothing purchases, and even the corrugated inserts of lightbulb cartons and cosmetic boxes.

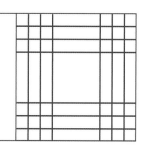

Search your community for other freebies. Several of the patterned papers in this book were found in discontinued wallpaper sample books about to be discarded by an interior design shop in my small town. Local printers, paper super-stores, and paper wholesalers might have outdated paper sample books that could be yours for the asking. After carefully removing the samples from the books (watch those staples), you will often find that the swatches are large enough to make complete projects.

THE WORK BOX

To complete the projects to come, you'll need a variety of easy-to-find supplies, which are listed below. Collect all of these pieces of basic equipment and stash them together in a toolbox, sturdy basket, tote bag, or plastic storage container. This will be your "Work Box." If there are little children in your home, be sure to keep your Work Box out of their reach. Every time you make a project you will need to use at least one item from the Work Box, so most of the tools and supplies listed here won't appear again on the materials list provided for each project.

Clip Clothespins

These are useful to hold glued pieces of paper together while they dry. Also, use clothespins as giant paper clips to keep your patterns, papers, and notes organized.

Compass

An ordinary pencil-holding compass is adequate for drawing circles. For the greatest cutting accuracy, however, an adjustable circle cutter is the best.

Cotton Swabs

Dampened just a little bit, a cotton swab is perfect for removing glue spots. Always test this on a piece of scrap paper. Cotton swabs also work as extensions of your finger-tips for flattening glue tabs inside three-dimensional forms.

Craft Knife and Replacement Blades

Scissors can be used for some of the projects, but many designs require the use of a craft knife with a No. 11 blade. Select a knife with a soft, rubberized (preferably contoured) barrel for comfort and control and an anti-roll device and cap for safety. The knife should also have a safe and easy blade-release mechanism.

In order to protect your most precious tools—your own two hands—avoid all other cutting devices. It's wise to keep an extra packet of replacement blades on hand.

Cutting Mat

The best cutting base has a translucent, semihard, rubberlike surface that accepts the blade and then miraculously heals itself. Choose a nonslip mat that is conveniently marked with a grid pattern. Heavy cardboard can be used as a temporary cutting mat, but it wears out quickly and dulls the blade of your craft knife. Some self-healing cutting mats are really made for rotary cutters, and they forget how to heal when a craft blade mars the surface.

Drawing Board (optional)

A drawing board with a T-square and triangles is not a must, but such supplies do ensure accuracy and efficiency. If you consider such a purchase, a plastic studio drawing board with a paper clamp and a removable transparent sliding straightedge that acts as a T-square is affordable and more than adequate. To complete the set, use inexpensive 45- and 60-degree plastic triangles on the board. Neither the plastic board nor the plastic triangles should be used with a craft knife.

Eraser

With gentle pressure, a nonabrasive white vinyl eraser removes pencil lines neatly, without smudging. For precise work, the most convenient form is a click eraser that resembles a mechanical pencil. The tip of a click eraser is a helpful tool when folding the points of stars. Use it to lift and roll the paper and to press the folds flat.

Folding Tool

A bone folder (a folding tool available at craft stores), a straight edge, or even an old spatula or wooden spoon can be dragged across a project to flatten it after folding or gluing. Work should always be protected with a cover sheet of clean scrap paper when this is done.

Glue

Purchase small-size glue sticks and keep a few extra new ones on hand because they dry out quickly. Elmer's All-Purpose Glue Stick dries clear and makes a strong bond. It also dries quickly but not instantly, so if you work fast, you can make small adjustments. Always try a test patch of glue on your good paper and allow it to dry.

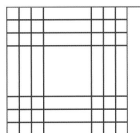

Graph Paper

Grid paper ensures accuracy when it is necessary to draw patterns by hand.

Monofilament

This soft, invisible, nylon sewing thread is used to make hanging loops for some of the ornament projects.

Needles and Pins

You'll need needles and pins to pierce holes in patterns so you can inconspicuously transfer construction details onto your good paper with tiny pencil dots. Sometimes both the pattern and the work are pierced simultaneously. "T" pins are a good choice because the bar at the top serves as a kind of handle, making the pin easy to hold. When piercing, use a self–healing cutting mat to protect the work surface.

Paper Clips

Use aluminum or coated paper clips to anchor a pattern in place or to hold together glued layers of paper while they dry. Use paper clips with a cover sheet to avoid scratching your work.

Paper Punches

Metal plier-type paper punches are readily available in ¹⁄₁₆-inch (1.6-mm), ⅛-inch (3.2-mm), and ¼-inch (6.4-mm) circle diameters. Decorative punches produce a variety of confetti shapes, such as hearts, flowers, and stars. Manufacturers suggest punching through waxed paper to lubricate the cutting mechanism and punching through aluminum foil to sharpen the edge of the blades. Now and then, in desperation, I have even cut through very fine sandpaper to sharpen a punch, but it's not recommended by manufacturers.

Pencils and Sharpener

Use a regular No. 2 pencil or a mechanical pencil with soft graphite lead to draw your own patterns and transfer dots from patterns to paper. Use a red pencil to highlight cutting lines or details on patterns. A quality handheld sharpener with a twist-off barrel for emptying shavings will help to keep your work area neat.

Ruler

A 12-inch (30.5-cm) and an 18-inch (45.7-cm) ruler are sufficient for most of the projects. A 6-inch (15.2-cm) ruler is nice to have when measuring on a very small format. A safety ruler serves double-duty as a measuring device and a straight-edge when cutting with a craft knife. Safety rulers have non-skid backings and are designed so there is a barrier between your fingers and the knife.

Scissors

When selecting scissors, consider comfort as well as size. Try them before you buy them. For general use, I favor lightweight, all-purpose, 7-inch (17.8-cm) scissors with molded plastic handles. For delicate and precise work, I use 5-inch (12.7-cm) pointed-tip embroidery scissors. You'll need paper edgers for cutting patches on some of the quilt cards. Dozens of designs are available, but only the scalloped and the zigzag edgers were used in this book.

Scrap Paper

Recycle the scraps of copy paper that are leftover after cutting out patterns. When it is necessary to make additional panels for card patterns, use scrap paper if graph paper is not available. While working with glue, use the larger pieces of leftover copy paper to protect the work surface. The smaller pieces can be used to mask glue-free areas on the work itself. To evenly distribute glue and sharply crease folding lines as well, cover the completed work with a piece of scrap paper before dragging a ruler or a bone folder over it. The clean, print-free side is the only surface of the copy paper that should touch the work.

Tape

You'll need traditional transparent tape occasionally to hold pieces together and to reinforce vulnerable scored lines. Removable tape is a necessity when making patterns and attaching them to good paper. Try the bright blue removable masking tape available in paint and hardware stores. Several types are offered, but only purchase the one that is labeled "for delicate surfaces." The manufacturer does not recommend this tape for use on paper, but it seems to work well. Always test before using questionable products. Another way to hold patterns and paper together is by using drafting dots, ⅞-inch (2.2-cm) diameter circles of removable tape, available in craft shops and art stores. Use foam tape to create a dimensional effect when stacking together the paper layers of a motif.

Toothpicks

When adding bits of glue in tight places, a toothpick is a helpful little tool.

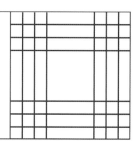

Tweezers

Use tweezers to move tiny pieces of paper into position and to hold hard-to-reach layers of glued paper together while drying.

PAPER QUILT CLASS

"If all else fails, read the directions." I don't know who first offered that sage advice, but I know many who take it to heart! The best lessons do sometimes come from our worst mistakes, but taking the time to review basic information at the beginning of an activity is a better way to learn, so please read on.

Getting Started

Beginning each paper quilt is somewhat like trying a new recipe, so first check the list of ingredients for availability, then read through the directions to gain a general understanding of the preparation ahead. Most of the quilt motifs are placed on square-format cards, easily made using the patterns and instructions. Square cards are visually pleasing, but square envelopes require extra postage, and must be at least 5 inches (12.7-cm) in size, too big for these designs. So, all the envelope patterns provided are rectangles.

Choosing Colors

If you don't believe that you have a good eye for color, build your confidence with the help of others who have color courage. Look for appealing patterned paper or fabric, take note of the color mix, and then re-create it with paper. When you start mixing and matching colors and patterns, you will most likely find unexpected combinations that you really like; clip them together in combos, reserving them for future projects. For the very best lessons in color theory, check with Mother Nature, the ultimate design consultant, who creates a new palette for every changing season. Inspiration is omnipresent in the natural world of flowers, foliage, water, rocks, trees, grass, and sky. In the commercial world, watch for innovative colorways on greeting cards, gift wraps, packaging, print advertising, and textiles. Accidental color spills from scraps that have fallen to the floor or been left on the drawing board could also inspire serendipitous combinations.

Preparing Paper

When making a multipaneled accordion-folded card, if text-weight duplex paper is not available in the size required, use one 8½- by 11-inch (21.6- by 27.9-cm) piece in its place. Cut the paper in the following way: one 4¼- by 8½-inch (10.8- by 21.6-cm) piece and one 4¼- by 8¾-inch (10.8- by 22.2-cm) piece. Place the pieces of paper side by side on the work surface so the inside color of the card faces up. On one 4¼-inch (10.8-cm) edge of the larger piece of paper, draw and score a pencil line ¼ inch (6.4mm) from the edge for a glue tab. Align one 4¼-inch (10.8-cm) edge of the smaller piece on the pencil line of the longer piece and glue the overlapped edges together.

To make your own duplex papers for any card, first cut and fold the basic card using one of the selected papers. Then, before cutting out the motif, cut the other selected paper into squares and glue it to the reverse side of the unfolded card. Both papers should be flush along the top and bottom edges, with a narrow space left between each panel so the card will fold well. This homemade duplex paper will be fine for cards with cut-out motifs, but it won't work well at all for motifs that are folded.

- Continuous solid lines are always cutting lines.
- Dotted lines show the placement of a detail or another piece of paper.
- Broken lines indicate folding lines.

Making Patterns

To save time and ensure accuracy, the projects here are best made using photocopies of patterns from the back of the book. Take note of the different kinds of lines on the patterns.

- Continuous solid lines are always cutting lines.
- Dotted lines show the placement of a detail or another piece of paper.
- Broken lines indicate folding lines.

When making a pattern photocopy, make an extra one if you are unsure about the construction of a project.

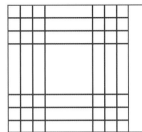

Use the extra copy to rehearse the assembly of the design, reserving your good paper until you are sure of the technique. Carefully measure the photocopied patterns to compare them in size to the patterns printed in the book; sometimes copiers make prints that are ⅛ inch (3.2mm) smaller or larger than the original. An oversized card might not fit inside the envelope size suggested in the Materials list for each project.

Transferring Details

Transfer pattern details onto your project by using a needle or a pin to pierce the pattern details, such as folding lines, before the pattern is placed on your project paper. The details can then be transferred directly from the pattern onto the project paper by placing pencil dots inside the pinholes. The directions for some projects suggest piercing the pattern and the paper at the same time without using a pencil.

Using Tape

Use removable tape or paper clips to hold patterns on your project paper; but first make a test patch of tape on a small section of your good paper to see if it mars the surface or leaves a sticky spot. Removable tape is easy to remove, but if it is left in place for even a short time, it will leave a sticky residue that is not easy to remove. When lifting tape from your work, gently pull it away from the edge of the project paper toward the work surface, not from the work surface toward the project.

Placing Motifs

To center a square motif on a square card, draw very light diagonal pencil lines from one corner to the opposite corner on the card front. Place the motif by matching each of its corners with the diagonal lines. Be mindful of the placement of cut-out motifs when writing a greeting inside a finished card—you don't want your message to interfere with the design. Sometimes the best place for a greeting is on the reverse side of the front panel or on the back of the card.

Erasing Drawings

Rough erasing will mar or tear the surface of some papers and remove the color or make shiny spots on others. Make slow gentle strokes in one direction instead of scrubbing the paper in a fury. Use a light touch when drawing so you won't need to erase heavy lines.

Cutting Papers

Practice cutting scrap paper with a craft knife, and find the way to hold it that gives you the greatest sense of comfort and control. To cut accurate lines of just the right length, put tiny red dots on the pattern at the beginning and end of each cutting line: Think of the dots as little stop signs to keep you from cutting too far.

To cut or score straight lines, always use a nonslip safety ruler or straightedge as a barrier between your fingers and the craft knife. When cutting or scoring curved lines, keep moving the paper, instead of the knife, and place your fingers away from the path of the blade. If working on a small piece of paper brings your hand too close to the knife, securely tape the small piece of paper onto a bigger piece.

When cutting multiple duplicate shapes together, stack the papers and use tape or clips to hold each layer of paper securely to the next. If the layers are not bound together, they will shift as pressure is applied on the knife, and the cutting will not be accurate. When cutting through multiple layers of paper, it is safer to make several successive cuts with gentle pressure rather than trying to cut through all the layers with one heavy-handed pass of the knife. It is hazardous to use a dull blade or one with even a tiny piece of the tip broken off. These conditions diminish your control of the knife and they might ruin the paper, tearing it instead of cutting it. After applying glue to paper, allow it to dry thoroughly before cutting it. Always keep your eyes and your full attention on the blade. Carefully wrap a used blade in tape before disposing of it responsibly.

For the greatest accuracy when cutting curves with scissors, keep the scissors stationary, and move the paper into the cutting blades, instead of keeping the paper stationary and moving the scissors around it.

Paper Punching

Sometimes paper punches make me crazy because they don't always cut well after just a few uses (page 14). When a punch is actually working well, cutting a few layers of paper together instead of a single piece often produces crisper edges. When punching fragile paper, first sandwich it between two layers of scrap paper.

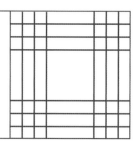

Scoring and Folding

Medium-weight and heavy paper must be scored in order to fold neatly. Move the craft knife along an accurately drawn folding line (the broken line on a pattern), making a very shallow groove in the paper without cutting through it. Within the groove, the knife breaks only the very top fibers of the paper, enabling you to fold it precisely. When scoring curved lines, move the paper instead of the knife as you follow the line. It is best to score small pieces before they are cut out.

Some projects require scoring on the front of the piece; others need scoring on the reverse side. The instructions will tell you when and where to score. Paper is usually bent away from a scored line.

Mountain Folds

When you see the term "mountain fold," mark and score the folding line on the paper, then bend the paper away from you to create the peak of an imaginary mountain.

Valley Folds

When you see the term "valley fold," mark and score the folding line on the reverse side of the paper, then flip the paper over to the right side and bend it toward you to make a little valley.

Making Accordion-Folded Paper

To create an accordion-folded piece of paper, make alternating parallel mountain and valley folds on it. To protect your paper, place a cover sheet of clean scrap paper over your work when creasing or flattening it.

Using Glue

Sometimes glue can change the color of a paper or bubble its surface, so always make a test patch on your good paper and allow it to dry thoroughly before you proceed. Spread a thin layer of glue quickly and uniformly, using a craft stick or folded index card as a tool, depending on the size of your work. After joining glued surfaces, place a clean cover sheet over the work to protect it, then rub the area to smooth it and distribute the glue. Do the smoothing with your fingertips, or roll a glue-stick tube on it, or pull a straightedge or bone folder over the work. Then remove the cover sheet and use paper clips or clothespins with a new cover sheet to hold the glued areas together until dry. Alternatively, sandwich the piece between two layers of scrap paper and place it under a stack of heavy books.

Elmer's All-Purpose Glue Stick dries clear, but if it leaves shiny spots, use a damp, not wet, cotton swab to carefully wipe away the dried glue. Keep the opposite cotton end dry so it can be used to smooth the dampened area and absorb excess moisture. First, try the dampened swab on a scrap piece to see if moisture mars the paper surface or causes the color to bleed. An eraser works well in removing residual glue on some papers and so does scraping the glue with the edge of an index card. Test every method before trying it on your good paper.

MAINTAINING SUPPLIES

Treat your paper collection with care. Store the sheets flat. You can make a hinged storage portfolio for large papers by using wide tape to join two same-sized pieces of cardboard together along one edge. Sort smaller pieces of paper by color in folders, bags, or envelopes, but before you tuck them away, remove all traces of tape and glue so the residue will not mar the texture or discolor the paper surface.

Rolling paper for storage is not a good idea, but if you absolutely must do it, roll the pieces very loosely and don't put rubber bands, tape, or paper clips on them. Instead, wrap a strip of scrap paper around the roll and use a piece of tape to attach the strip to itself. If paper is difficult to flatten after being rolled, gently roll it in the opposite direction.

Keep paper out of the sun and away from moisture and make sure your hands are very clean and dry before you touch it. Dust, fingerprints, and graphite smudges are difficult to remove; color fading is irreversible. Some papers absorb ambient moisture on humid days. As a result, they tear very easily when being cut with a craft knife. To avoid this disappointment, give the paper a brief encounter with a hair dryer. Then use a sharp new blade to cut slowly across the paper while pressing the flattest side of the straightedge firmly against the cutting line.

Although it is easier said than done, keep your work area neat and clean. Only set up the items you need for the project at hand, and keep your tools clean, too. Replace the cap on the glue. Store your tapes in plastic bags to keep the edges clean. Wash your hands after using pencils and glue. And don't use your drawing board for a snack tray!

2

SQUARE ON SQUARE

A square is the most basic and simple of patchwork shapes. It was the pattern of choice in the late eighteenth century when the good parts of worn out clothing were salvaged and cut into patches for utilitarian scrap quilts. An easy pattern for beginners, the square motif was most often used for everyday one-patch quilts instead of the multipatch "best" quilts reserved for guests and special occasions. Beginner or expert, this chapter is a great place to start making your first paper quilt cards!

Gordian Knot Design 2 (page 30)

SQUARE ON SQUARE

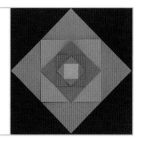

One of my old quilt books lists this Square on Square design as The Boxes Quilt. Seeing that name made me think of the delightful custom of wrapping gift boxes within gift boxes, each to be opened with great anticipation until the real gift is finally revealed inside the last tiny box. When this quilt design is interpreted with square upon square of folded paper, it's fun to play with the folds and arrange the papers in various combinations, creating ever-changing kaleidoscopes of color, pattern, and form.

MATERIALS

For one 4" (10.2-cm) square card

Photocopy of the pattern, page 107

Equipment in the Work Box, pages 13–15

4 by 8" (10.2 by 20.4-cm) piece of card-stock, scored and folded to make a 4" (10.2-cm) square card

Six squares of text paper in a variety of colors: 3½" (8.9-cm); 2¾" (7.0-cm); 2½" (6.4-cm); 1¾" (4.4-cm); 1½" (3.8-cm); 1" (2.5-cm)

Envelope, 4¼ by 5⅛" (10.8 by 13.0-cm), or Envelope A pattern, page 104, and instructions, pages 103–104

Square on Square Card

INSTRUCTIONS

1. On the card front, use a sharp pencil and a straightedge to draw very light lines diagonally from corner to corner so they intersect at the center of the square.

2. Great accuracy is required when cutting, folding, and placing each paper square. Tape the largest square on a protected work surface. Tape the rough-cut full pattern of concentric squares on top. Cut out Square 1 right through the pattern. Remove and reserve the pattern. Lightly draw the diagonals on Square 1 and make a tiny pinhole where the lines intersect at the center (Drawing 1).

3. Flip Square 1 over to the reverse (unmarked) side. Fold one corner tip exactly to the center pinhole, crease it sharply, and unfold (Drawing 2). Fold the next corner to the pinhole and unfold it. Repeat with the remaining two corners. Unfold Square 1 and flip it over to the pencil-marked side of the paper. Place a tiny pinhole exactly where each pencil line intersects each folding line (Drawing 3). Erase the pencil lines.

Flip Square 1 over to the reverse side, fold it again on the original folding lines, and put it aside.

4. Using the reserved pattern, refer to Steps 2 and 3 to cut the five remaining Squares 2–6. Referring to Step 3, draw the diagonals and fold all of the squares except the smallest one (Square 6). Square 5 needs no pinholes on the folding lines. Square 6 needs no pinholes or folds at all.

5. Place the small flat Square 6 within the center of unfolded Square 5. Check the size and fit by folding the corner flaps of Square 5 over Square 6. Trim Square 6 slightly, if necessary. Glue Square 6 at the center of unfolded Square 5. When dry, fold the flaps of Square 5 over Square 6. Spread glue on the reverse side of folded Square 5 and center it diagonally on unfolded Square 4. The tips of the folded corners of Square 5 should align precisely with the pinholes on Square 4. Continue gluing the remaining folded squares within the larger unfolded squares. Spread glue on the reverse side of folded Square 1, center it on the card front, and allow it to dry.

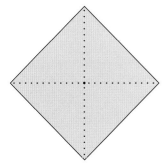

1. Draw the diagonals and mark the center of the square with a pinhole.

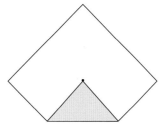

2. Fold each corner of the square to the center pinhole.

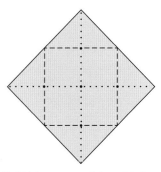

3. Unfold the square and place pinholes at the points where the pencil lines intersect the folding lines.

DOUBLE IRISH CHAIN

There are Single Irish Chains, Double Irish Chains, and Triple Irish Chains. I don't know why the chains are Irish, but I do know that the patterns for them were very popular with Colonial quilters. When you cut this design from a four-panel card, save all the cut-outs and you'll be able to double your Double Irish Chain. Just stack the leftover pieces, then center and glue them to the front of a two-panel card or the top of a small gift box.

MATERIALS

For one 4¼" (10.8-cm) square card

Four photocopies of the pattern, page 106

Equipment in the Work Box, pages 13–15

4¼ by 17" (10.8 by 43.2-cm) piece of text-weight, duplex paper

2½" (6.4-cm) square of contrasting text paper for the back of Panel 3

2½" (6.4-cm) square of text paper that matches the outside of the card for the back of Panel 4

Envelope, 4⅜ by 5¾" (11.1 by 14.6-cm), or Envelope B pattern, page 105, and instructions, pages 103–104

Note: If text-weight duplex paper is unavailable in the size required, substitute one 8½ by 11" (21.6 by 27.9-cm) piece of duplex paper and refer to A Paper Primer on page 12.

INSTRUCTIONS

1. Precisely cut the pattern from each of the four copies. Label them A, B, C, and D. Tape them together in ABCD order (Drawing 1) to make a full pattern for the inside of the unfolded card.

2. Indicate the shaded cutting area on each panel with a pencil (Drawing 2).

3. Accordion-fold the pattern into the 4¼" (10.8-cm) square (Drawing 3) so all the motifs are inside the pattern. Hold the folded pattern against a sunny window to check the alignment of the card edges and the motif on each panel. Adjust if necessary.

4. Lightly score and accordion-fold the duplex paper, then unfold it. Place the paper on the work surface so the inside of the card (green in the photo) is facing up. Label the panels, A, B, C, and D (Drawing 2).

Flip the paper over so the outside surface (cream in the photo) is facing up and the panels are in DCBA order (Drawing 4). Center and glue the contrasting 2½" (6.4-cm) square (red in the photo) to Panel C.

5. Flip the paper over again and tape it to the work surface so the inside of the card (green) is facing up and the contrasting square (red) is behind Panel C. With Panel A on the left, tape the pattern on top of the card. Cutting directly through the pattern and the card, cut out the shaded motifs on Panels A, B, C, and D, and reserve the pieces. Remove the pattern. Glue the remaining 2½" (6.4-cm) square behind Panel 4 so the center motif is the same color as the card front.

6. To make Card Design 2, stack, center, and glue together the reserved cut-out pieces. Glue the unit to the front of a 4¼" (10.8-cm) square card, first backing it with a contrasting border square, if desired.

(L to R): Card Design 2, Card Design 1

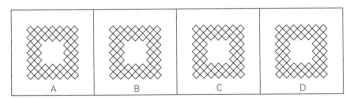

1. Tape four photocopies together to make a pattern for the inside of the unfolded card.

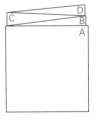

3. Accordion-fold the pattern and check for alignment of the motifs.

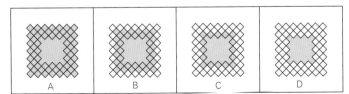

2. Add color to the shaded areas to indicate the cutting area on each panel.

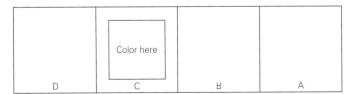

4. Flip the paper over so the outside surface of the card faces up.

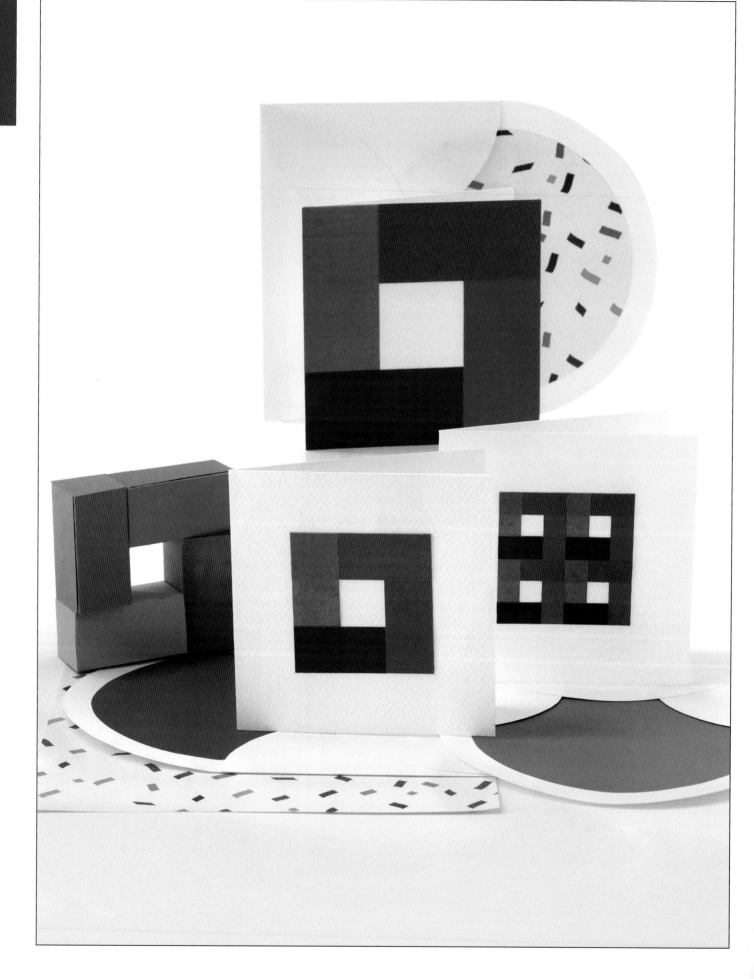

BRIGHT HOPES

To create the Bright Hopes motif, overlap razzle-dazzle rectangles—the brighter, the better—around a small center square. Copy the pattern guide and use it as a foundation, gluing the paper patches right on top of it, before placing the completed motif on the card. There's a cluster box pattern here, too, just waiting to be enlarged to any size at all.

MATERIALS

card design 1 or card design 2

For one 4¼" (10.8-cm) square card

Photocopy of the patterns and pattern guides for Design 1 or Design 2, page 107

Equipment in the Work Box, pages 13–15

4¼ by 8½" (10.8 by 21.6-cm) piece of cardstock, scored and folded to make a 4¼" (10.8-cm) square card

Four different 3" (7.6) squares of brightly-colored text paper for Design 1 or Design 2

Envelope, 4⅜ by 5¾" (11.1 by 14.6-cm), or Envelope B, pattern, page 105, and instructions, pages 103–104

cluster box

Materials for one 3" by 3" by 1" (7.6 by 7.6 by 2.5-cm) box

Four photocopies of the box pattern

Equipment in the Work Box, pages 13–15

Four 5½" (14.0-cm) squares of cardstock, each a different color

Note: No patterns are needed to produce Card Design 3. First cut four 1⅜ by 4¼" (3.5 by 10.8-cm) rectangles of text paper. Then, referring to the photograph, overlap and glue the rectangles around the edges of a 4¼" (10.8-cm) card.

Top: Card Design 3 (see note); Bottom (L to R): Cluster Box, Card Design 1, Card Design 2

INSTRUCTIONS

card design 1

1. Rough-cut the pattern guide and the pattern for the patches for Design 1.

2. Tape together the four text paper squares. Tape the patch pattern on top of the stack. Cut the patches all at once, directly through the pattern. Determine the color arrangement and place a number, 1–4, on the reverse side of each patch to identify the location of each color on the pattern guide.

3. Overlap and glue each patch in place on the pattern guide. When the glue is dry, cut out the center square and trim away the rough-cut edges of the pattern guide. Center and glue the block on the card front.

card design 2

1. Rough-cut the pattern guide and the pattern for the patches for Design 2.

2. Tape together the four text papers, then tape the patch pattern on top of the stack. Cut the patches all at once, right through the pattern. On the reverse side of each different colored patch, place a number 1–4. There will be two patches of each color.

3. On the pattern guide, place one tiny spot of glue on each dot. Place the vertical colors 1, and 3, on the pattern guide (Drawing 1).

When the glue is dry, weave in the horizontal colors 2 and 4, passing them under and over 1 and 3. Glue the patches in place (Drawing 2). Cut out the center squares and trim away the rough edges on the pattern guide. Center and glue the block on the card front.

cluster box

1. Rough-cut each of the four box patterns. Tape each pattern to one of the cardstock squares.

2. Cut right through the pattern to cut out each color box piece. Score the folding lines.

3. After prefolding each box piece into shape, apply glue to the tabs where indicated and form each box. Allow the glue to dry.

4. On a piece of scrap paper, draw a 3" (7.6-cm) square with a 1" (2.5-cm) square at the center of it.

5. Using the scrap paper square as a guide, glue the boxes together in the Bright Hopes format. The hinge edge of every box should surround the center square. Glue each box to its neighbor, but not to the scrap paper square below it. Use several not-too-tight rubber bands to hold the boxes together as the glue dries.

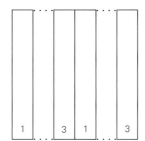

1. Glue vertical colors 1 and 3 on the Design 2 pattern guide.

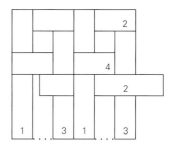

2. Weave horizontal patches 2 and 4 and glue them in place on the Design 2 pattern guide.

ECONOMY PATCH

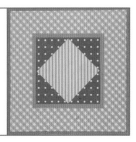

My grandmother, who favored "leftover" patterns like this, and even patched the patches on her quilts, preached the essence of economy: "Use it up. Wear it out. Make it do, or do without." Economy Patch is a pleasing, basic design offering the opportunity to combine a hodgepodge of decorative paper scraps. When four Economy motifs are grouped together, they create the Star and Block design. So, in addition to the card projects, a pattern for a Star and Block Box is also provided.

MATERIALS

Common materials for one 4¼" (10.8-cm) square card, Design 1 or 2

Equipment in the Work Box, pages 13–15

4¼ by 8½" (10.8 by 21.6-cm) piece of card stock, scored and folded to make a 4¼" (10.8-cm) square card

Envelope, 4⅜ by 5¾" (11.1 by 14.6-cm), or Envelope B pattern, page 105, and instructions, pages 103–104

additional materials for design 1

Photocopy of the Design 1 pattern, page 108

4" (10.2-cm) square of duplex text-weight or origami paper for the motif

2½" (6.4-cm) square of paper for border

additional materials for design 2

4" (10.2-cm) square of paper for the wide motif border

2½" (6.4-cm) square of paper for the narrow motif border

2¼" (5.7-cm) square of paper for the motif

1⁷⁄₁₆" (3.7-cm) square of paper for the diagonal motif center

Left top: Economy Patch Box; Left bottom: Star and Block Box; Right top: Card Design 1; Right bottom: Card Design 2

INSTRUCTIONS
card design 1

1. Rough-cut around the block pattern. Select the color desired for the small diagonal squares of the motif (blue in the photo); tape the pattern to that side of the paper. Make a tiny pinhole at the end of each diagonal line, through both pattern and paper.

2. Leaving the pattern in place and using a new blade, cut each diagonal crossed line very accurately, right through the pattern. Cut around the pattern edges and leave the paper with the same color facing up.

3. Refer to the pattern and lightly score the broken lines that make a square around each of the diagonally cut lines. The scored lines should run from pinhole to pinhole. Each diagonally cut line should touch a pinhole. Make adjustments if necessary.

4. Flip the paper to the reverse side. Push each little triangle up from the back and fold it down to make a tiny square opening framed by a diagonal square that is in contrast to the background (Drawing 1). Center and glue the motif on the border paper. Then center and glue the motif unit on the card front.

card design 2

1. No patterns are necessary because the components have been precut to size. Center and glue the 1⁷⁄₁₆" (3.7-cm) center square diagonally on the 2¼" (5.7-cm) square. Center and glue the motif unit on the 2½" (6.4-cm) square to make a narrow border around it. Allow the glue to dry.

2. Center and glue the motif unit on the 4" (10.2-cm) square and then center and glue that combined unit on the card front.

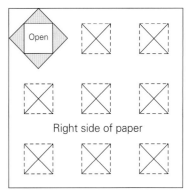

Right side of paper

1. For Design 1, push the cut area up from the back to open the center square and fold back the little triangles to form a diagonal square around the opening.

ECONOMY PATCH

MATERIALS

economy patch box

For one 2" (5.1-cm) box

Photocopy of the Economy Patch Box pattern, page 108

Equipment in the Work Box, pages 13–15

7 by 9" (17.8 by 22.9-cm) piece of duplex paper

Six 1⅞" (4.8-cm) paper squares for the box lining

star and block box

For one 2" (5.1-cm) box

Photocopy of the patterns for the Economy Patch Box and the Star and Block Substitute Box Top, page 108

Equipment in the Work Box, pages 13–15

7 by 9" (17.8 by 22.9-cm) piece of duplex paper

1⅞" (4.8-cm) paper square for box top lining

INSTRUCTIONS

economy patch box

1. Rough-cut the pattern. Tape it to the side of the paper that will be inside the box.

2. Cut right through the pattern, cutting the crossed diagonal lines very carefully. Before cutting, make a tiny pinhole at the end of each crossed line for guidance. Cut out the box shape.

3. Still working on the inside surface of the box, refer to the pattern and score all the broken lines that make a square around each pair of diagonal cut lines. The scored lines should run from pinhole to pinhole. The ends of each diagonal cut line should touch a pinhole. Make adjustments if necessary.

4. Flip the paper to the reverse side (the outside box surface). Score and crease the box folding lines. Working from the back, push up each cut area to open the center square, and fold back the little triangles like shutters to create a diagonal square around the opening. Glue the triangles flat against the box if desired.

5. On the right side of each lining piece, spread a thin line of glue around the edges. Center and place a lining piece behind each panel.

star and block box

1. Rough-cut the Economy Patch Box pattern (page 108). Precisely cut out the Substitute Box Top and glue it in place on the box top portion of the Economy Patch pattern. Tape the pattern to the surface of the paper that will be inside the box.

2. Complete Steps 2–4 of the Economy Patch Box instructions, cutting only the substitute top panel of the box, not the other panels. On the right side of the lining piece, spread a thin line of glue around the edges. Center and place the lining inside the box top.

Card Tricks: The House That Jack Built

To speed-build a house for Jack, simply cut a square of striped paper into quarter sections and arrange the small patches diagonally on a background square. For more control over the placement of the stripes, substitute a strip of vertically striped paper and slice off four squares for the card. The House That Jack Built was originally published by *The Ladies Art Company,* the first mail-order quilt pattern company, established in 1890.

MATERIALS

For one 4¼" (10.8-cm) card

Equipment in the Work Box, pages 13–15

4¼ by 8½" (10.8 by 21.6-cm) piece of cardstock, scored and folded to make a 4 ¼" (10.8-cm) square card

3¼" (8.3-cm) square of scrap paper for the pattern guide

3¾" (9.5-cm) square of paper for the background square

3½" (8.9-cm) square of paper for the first border, optional

3¾" (9.5-cm) square of paper for the second border, optional

Striped paper: Either a 2¼" (5.7-cm) square, or a 1⅛ by 6" (2.9 by 15.2-cm) rectangle, cut so the stripes are parallel to the length

Envelope, 4⅜ by 5¾ (11.1 by 14.6-cm), or Envelope B pattern, page 105, and instructions, pages 103–104

INSTRUCTIONS

1. No patterns are needed. Make the four 1⅛" (2.9-cm) squares by either cutting the large striped square into quarter sections, or slicing 1⅛" (2.9-cm) squares from the strip of paper. Put the squares aside.

2. To make a placement guide for the background square, fold the scrap paper square as follows. Fold the square in half horizontally, then unfold it. Fold the top and bottom edges of the square to meet the center folding line and unfold them, making four equal horizontal sections divided by three folding lines. Rotate the square 45-degrees and repeat the process to make a folded grid of sixteen squares. Unfold the placement guide, precisely place three tiny dots on each edge of the square to mark the folding lines, and put it aside.

3. Pencil-draw a 3¼" (8.3-cm) square at the center of the background paper and tape the unfolded placement guide precisely on top of the pencil-drawn square. Use a very sharp pencil to carefully mark each edge of the square that is drawn on the background paper with the three dots drawn on each edge of the placement guide. Remove the pattern and connect the dots with light pencil lines to re-create a grid on the background square.

4. Refer to the photo for the placement of the reserved striped squares and glue them in place on the background square. Trim the edges of the background, if necessary. Gently erase the pencil lines. Center and glue the motif directly onto the card or first center and glue it on the optional border papers, trimming the width of each border to suit the width of the stripes.

GORDIAN KNOT

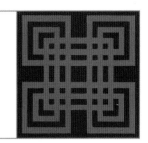

Greek legend tells the tale of the knot with no visible ends. The one to untie the knot would become the ruler of Asia. Alexander the Great solved the dilemma by cutting the knot with his sword. From that time, the Gordian Knot has symbolized an extremely complicated problem solved by drastic means. Stitching the Gordian Knot design does indeed look extremely complicated, but cutting it in paper isn't difficult at all.

MATERIALS

Common materials for one 4¼" (10.8-cm) square card, Design 1 or 2

Equipment in the Work Box, pages 13–15

4¼ by 8½" (10.8 by 21.6-cm) piece of cardstock, scored, and folded to make a 4¼" (10.8-cm) square card

4" (10.2-cm) square of paper for the front panel

Envelope, 4⅜ by 5¾" (11.1 by 14.6-cm), or Envelope B pattern, page 105, and instructions, pages 103–104

additional materials for design 1

Photocopy of the pattern, page 109

2⅞" (7.3-cm) square of paper for the center motif

2⅞" (7.3-cm) square of paper for the border around the center motif

additional materials for design 2

Four photocopies of pattern, page 109

Three different 3" (7.6-cm) squares of text paper

INSTRUCTIONS

design 1

1. Cut around the pattern copy, trimming it fairly close to the center motif outline. Glue the pattern to the reverse side of the motif paper and put it aside until dry.

2. Glue and center the 4" (10.2-cm) square of paper on the card front. A narrow border of the card color will surround the edge.

3. To make the cutting lines of the motif copy clear, shade the knot with a pencil or a pen. Using a straightedge and a brand new blade, cut right through the copy to completely cut out the motif. The piece will be quite fragile.

4. Carefully spread glue on the reverse side of the design (the copy side) and center the knot on the motif border square. When dry, glue and center the border square on the card front.

design 2

1. Cut around each of the pattern copies, trimming close to the motif outline. To make the cutting lines of the copied motifs clear, number and shade the motifs for Layers 1, 2, and 3 (Drawings 1, 2, and 3).

2. To create a pattern of illusion, use the darkest paper for Layer 1 and the lightest paper for Layer 3. Tape one pattern onto each 3" (7.6-cm) square. Using a straight edge and a brand new knife blade and cutting right through the photocopy, completely cut out each color layer of the motif.

3. Glue and center the 4" (10.2-cm) square of paper on the card front. A narrow border of the card color will surround the edge. Trim the remaining photocopy precisely on the card outline. Center and clip the pattern on the front of the card. Make a tiny pinhole to transfer each corner circled on Drawing 4. Remove the pattern.

4. Carefully spread glue on the reverse side of Layer 1 and center it on the card front using the pinholes for placement guidelines. Follow the same procedure to add Layer 2 precisely on top of Layer 1, then add Layer 3.

Top: Card Design 2 (white variation); Bottom: Card Design 1, Card Design 2 (black variation)

1. Shade the pattern for Layer 1.

2. Shade the pattern for Layer 2.

3. Shade the pattern for Layer 3.

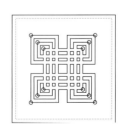

4. Mark each circled corner with a tiny pinhole.

INTERLOCKED SQUARES

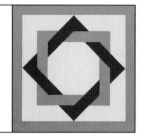

Once I cut the pieces for the Interlocked Squares Card, the design quickly evolved into some other familiar patterns. The individual links combined to make a garland resembling the patches on a Chain quilt. The little squares cut from the center of each link brought the Kite-Tail motif to mind and yet another garland was made from *those* leftovers. Using a square paper punch of any size is another quick and easy way to make the Kite Tail garland if you're out of leftovers.

MATERIALS

Common materials for one 4¼" (10.8-cm) square card, Design 1 or Design 2

4¼ by 8½" (10.8 by 21.6-cm) piece of cardstock, scored and folded to make a 4¼" (10.8-cm) square card

Photocopy of the pattern and pattern guide on 106

Equipment in the Work Box, pages 13–15

Two contrasting 2½" (6.4-cm) squares of paper for the interlocked squares

Envelope, 4⅜ by 5¾" (11.1 by 14.6-cm) or Envelope B pattern, page 105, and instructions, pages 103–104

additional materials for design 1

2½" (6.4-cm) square of white paper for the motif background

3" (7.6-cm) square of contrasting paper for the motif border

additional materials for design 2

2½" (6.4-cm) square of white paper for the motif diagonal background

3½" (8.9-cm) square of contrasting paper for the motif border

materials for chain garland and kite tail garland

For one 39" (99-cm) Chain Garland and one 19" (48.3-cm) Kite Tail Garland

Three photocopies of the garland pattern, page 106

Equipment in the Work Box, pages 13–15

Three 5½ by 6¾" (14.0 by 17.1-cm) coordinating pieces of cardstock

Paper punch, ¼ or ⅜" (6.4 or 9.5-mm) diameter circle or square

INSTRUCTIONS

card design 1 or design 2

1. Rough-cut the card pattern guide and set it aside. Rough-cut the card link pattern fairly close to the edges.

2. Stack and tape together the two contrasting 2½" (6.4-cm) motif squares. Tape the card link pattern on the top of the stack. Make tiny pinholes through the pattern to transfer the matching dots and the short cutting line to the papers. Cut right through the pattern to make two square links.

3. To make one link suitable for wrapping around the other, slice one on the short cutting line indicated on the pattern. Refer to the pattern guide to intertwine the two links, weaving the sliced link around the unsliced one. Conceal the slice under an overlapped area of the two links.

4. Use a pencil to mark the midpoint with a dot along each edge of the white 2½" (6.4-cm) background square. Glue the interlocked links in place on the background, carefully aligning all the matching dots. Each dot on the edge of one color link should tuck into a corner of the other color link. Likewise, each corner of one color link should touch one of the midpoint dots drawn on the edges of the background square. Use the pattern guide for guidance.

5. Refer to the photo to complete Design 1 or Design 2. Stack, center, and glue the motif on the proper border square. Glue the unit on the card front.

chain garland

1. Rough-cut around each of the three photocopied patterns. Tape one on each of the coordinating pieces of cardstock. First, cut the center squares and reserve them for the Kite Tail Garland or another project. Next, slice all the "cut" lines. Finally, cut out the square links.

2. Interlock the links, alternating the colors. Punch out twelve circles or squares of each color. Glue them in place to cover the slice on each matching link.

kite tail garland

1. Gather center square cut-outs from the Interlocked Squares Chain Garland to make a 19" (48.3-cm) Kite Tail.

2. Simply sandwich a continuous length of monofilament between two glued-together squares, placed diagonally, end to end.

Top (L to R): Interlocked Squares Ornament, Kite Tail Garland, Chain Garland; Bottom (L to R): Card Design 1, Card Design 2

3

CIRCLE UPON CIRCLE

Although they are quite easy to glue together on a paper quilt, circles and curved patches are more difficult to sew together than straight-sided squares and triangles. Considerable skill and infinite patience are required to stitch rounded pieces into patchworks. An equally-challenging alternative for stitching curved patterns is appliqué, created when the edges of cut-out shapes, such as leaves, are tucked under and sewn to a background fabric with nearly invisible stitches. Circles or sections of circles are often used to make pictorial patterns like flowers, suns, moons, and stars, and you will find several of those designs in the pages of this chapter.

Petal Circle in a Square (page 40)

CIRCLE UPON CIRCLE

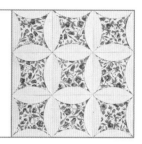

Circle Upon Circle, Tea Leaf, Orange Peel, Bay Leaf, Melon Patch, Flower Petals, New Moon, Compass, Pincushion, Mutual Benefit, Lover's Knot, and Save a Piece are just a few of the more than twenty names listed for this versatile pattern. Paper-punched circles are folded into squares to make the individual patches for the four design variations pictured here.

MATERIALS

For one 4¼" (10.8-cm) square card, Design 1, 2, 3, or 4

Equipment in the Work Box, pages 13–15

4¼ by 8½" (10.8 by 21.6-cm) piece of cardstock, scored and folded to make a 4¼" (10.8-cm) square card

Paper punch: 1½" (3.8-cm) circle

Nine 2" (5.1-cm) scraps of duplex origami-weight paper

3¼" (8.3-cm) square of paper for the base

Envelope, 4⅜ by 5¾" (11.1 by 14.6-cm), or Envelope B pattern, page 105, and instructions, pages 103–104

Note: Design 4, Bay Leaf, requires a 4⁵⁄₁₆" (10.9-cm) square card.

GENERAL INSTRUCTIONS

1. Use light pencil lines to draw diagonal lines from corner to corner across the card front and put the card aside.

2. Punch out nine circles. Fold each circle into a square, sharply creasing each folding line (Drawing 1, A–F). If the papers are difficult to fold in Drawing 1E, lightly score the folding lines.

3. Fold the motif base paper diagonally in each direction. Glue the first patch at the center of the motif base using the diagonal lines for guidance. Each corner of the patch should touch a folding line on the motif base. Glue the remaining patches in place. Trim the edges of the motif base if necessary.

Top: Design 2, Tea Leaf; Middle (L to R): Design 1, Circle Upon Circle; Design 4, Bay Leaf; Bottom: Design 3, Orange Peel

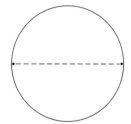

1A. Fold the circle in half and unfold it. Place a dot precisely at each end of the folding line on the front.

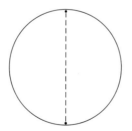

1B. Rotate the circle so the folding line is in a vertical position.

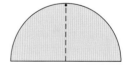

1C. Fold the circle in half again, aligning the dots at the ends of the first folding line.

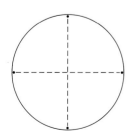

1D. Unfold the circle. Place a dot precisely at each end of the new folding line on the front and back.

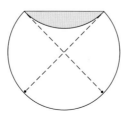

1E. Rotate the circle so the folding lines form an X. Fold down the top of the circle between the two dots to create one edge of the square.

1F. Continue to rotate and fold the circle until a square is formed.

instructions continue on next page

CIRCLE UPON CIRCLE

INSTRUCTIONS (continued)

design 1, circle upon circle

Complete Steps 1–3, page 37. Center and glue the complete motif on a 4⅛" (10.5-cm) square of paper before centering and gluing the unit on the card.

design 2, tea leaf

Complete Steps 1 and 2, page 37, preparing only one patch for the center of the Tea Leaf motif in the usual way with all the circle edges folded forward (Drawing 1A–1F). Then make four corner patches (Drawing 2) folding two circle edges forward and two back. Prepare four patches for the side edges of the motif (Drawing 3), folding three circle edges forward and one back. Complete Step 3, page 37. For a narrow border around the motif base, glue it to a 3³⁄₁₆" (8.1-cm) square. Then glue the motif unit to a 4⅛" (10.5-cm) square of decorative paper and glue the combined unit to the card.

design 3, orange peel

Complete Steps 1–3, page 37, punching and folding three extra circles. Cut two of the extra circles in half, then unfold them. Use one semicircle to make each extended scalloped corner (Drawing 4), gluing the pieces behind the motif. Unfold the one remaining circle and cut it into quarter sections (Drawing 5). Use one section to make a scallop on each edge of the motif (Drawing 5), and glue it in place. Referring to the photo on page 34 for placement, center and glue the motif on a 4" (10.2-cm) square, then on a 4⅛" (10.5-cm) square, and finally on the card front.

design 4, bay leaf

Complete Steps 1–3, page 37. Draw horizontal and vertical lines intersecting at the center of a 4⁵⁄₁₆" (11.0-cm) square card. Glue the motif in place diagonally on the card, using the crossed lines for guidance.

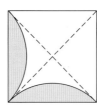
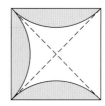

2. Fold back two adjacent circle edges to make a corner patch for Tea Leaf, Card Design 2.

3. Fold back one circle edge to make a side patch for Tea Leaf, Card Design 2.

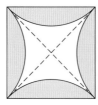

4. Combine one semicircle and one square patch to make a scalloped corner patch for Orange Peel, Design 3.

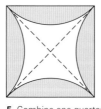
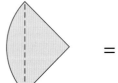
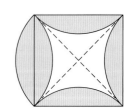

5. Combine one quarter-circle and one square patch to make a scalloped side patch for Orange Peel, Design 3.

Card Tricks: Moon Over the Mountain

This is a fun-to-do picture block! It's very quick and easy and provides a way to combine odd scraps of plain and fancy paper. The proportions of this pattern are very pleasing. The moon circle is centered on the sky square. The mountain triangle is equal to a quarter section of the sky, and the top of the mountain touches the center of the moon.

MATERIALS

For one 4¼" (10.8-cm) square card

Equipment in the Work Box, pages 13–15

2⅛" (5.4-cm) square of paper for the motif border, optional

2" (5.1-cm) square of paper for the sky background

1 by 2" (2.5 by 5.1-cm) piece of paper for the mountain

1⅛" (2.9-cm) diameter circle for the moon

4¼ by 8½" (10.8 by 21.6-cm) piece of cardstock, scored and folded to make a 4¼" (10.8-cm) square card

Envelope, 4⅜ by 5¾" (11.1 by 14.6-cm), or Envelope B pattern, page 105, and instructions, pages 103–104

INSTRUCTIONS

1. Draw light diagonal lines across the card front. Center and glue the optional motif border on the card. Each corner of the border square should touch a diagonal line. Center and glue the sky square on the border square, or glue it directly to the card if there is no border.

2. Fold and cut the mountain paper (Drawing 1–3). Glue the moon circle behind the mountain, aligning the center point of the moon with the tip of the mountain, and glue the unit to the lower edge of the sky square.

1. Place a dot midway along the top and bottom edges of the paper.

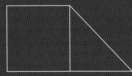

2. Fold each top corner diagonally, bringing it down to meet the midway dot on the lower edge. Crease sharply.

3. Trim off each corner, leaving a triangular mountain, or glue it in place folded as is.

PETAL CIRCLE IN A SQUARE

While this design is more than fifty years old, it is relatively new in the annals of quiltmaking history. The simple daisy motif is a fresh symbol for springtime greetings and it makes a nice box top, too. Scrapbooking paper is a good choice for the box. Avoid heavy cardstock because the lid and the base will be difficult to assemble and too chubby to fit together with ease.

MATERIALS

petal circle in a square card

For one 4¼" (10.8-cm) square card

Four photocopies of the pattern, page 110

Equipment in the Work Box, pages 13–15

4¼ by 17" (10.8 by 43.2-cm) piece of duplex paper

3" (7.6-cm) square of contrasting paper (blue in the photo) for the back of Panel 3

4¼" (10.8-cm) square of paper for the frame on the card front

Envelope, 4⅜ by 5¾" (11.1 by 14.6-cm), or Envelope B pattern, page 105, and instructions, pages 103–104

(L to R): Petal Circle in a Square Card, Petal Circle in a Square Boxes

INSTRUCTIONS

petal circle in a square card

1. To make the card pattern, precisely cut the 4¼" (10.8-cm) square from each of the four photocopies. Label the copies A, B, C, and D. Tape them together, in ABCD order (Drawing 1, page 43, top). This will be the pattern for the inside of the unfolded card. To indicate the cutting area on each panel of the pattern, use a pencil or a marker to add color to the shaded areas as shown. The shaded area on Panel D will be cut out of the pattern, not the card.

2. Accordion-fold the pattern into the 4¼" (10.8-cm) format (Drawing 2, page 43, top). All the design motifs will be inside the pattern. Hold the folded pattern against a sunny window to check the alignment of the card edges and the design motifs on each panel. Make adjustments if necessary. Cut out the entire shaded flower motif on Panel D, but do not cut the other pattern panels.

3. Lightly score and accordion-fold the duplex paper and unfold it (Drawing 2). Place the paper on the work surface so the inside surface of the card (white in the photo) is facing up. Discreetly label the panels, A, B, C, and D (Drawing 1). Flip the card paper over so the outside surface of the card is facing up (green in the photo) and the panels are in DCBA order. Center and glue the contrasting 3" (7.6-cm) square (blue in the photo) on this side of Panel C.

4. Flip the card paper over again and tape it to the work surface so the inside surface of the card (white) is facing up. Be sure that the contrasting square (blue) is behind Panel C. With Panel A on the left, tape the pattern on top of the card paper. Cutting directly through the pattern and the card paper, cut out the shaded design motifs on Panels A, B, and C only. Reserve the cut out flower and the flower pattern from Panel B. Lightly draw within the pre-cut area of the pattern on panel D, but do not cut the cardstock.

5. Remove the pattern. On Panel D, lightly draw diagonal lines from corner to corner and put the card aside. Clip the reserved flower pattern to the reserved flower cut-out. Cut the flower into four tulip-shaped sections (Drawing 3, page 43, top). Using the pencil lines on Panel D for guidance, glue the four tulip sections in place. Accordion-fold the card. Cut a 2½" (6.4-cm) square from the center of the 4¼" (10.8-cm) square frame paper, then center and glue the frame on the card front.

PETAL CIRCLE IN A SQUARE

MATERIALS

petal circle in a square box

For one 2½ by 2½ by ¾" (6.4 by 6.4 by 1.9-cm) box

Two photocopies of the box base, page 110

Two photocopies of the box lid, page 111

Photocopy of the box flower and flower center, page 111

Equipment in the Work Box, pages 13–15

6 by 12" (15.2 by 30.5-cm) piece of text paper for the box

3" (7.6-cm) square of duplex paper for the flower (white on one side)

Two 1½" (3.8-cm) squares of duplex paper for the flower center (white on one side)

3" (7.6-cm) square of paper for the circle

Note: Both the base and the lid are cut, scored, folded, and assembled in the same manner. However, the center square and dimensions of the base unit are smaller than the lid unit so that the lid and base will fit together. Before using good paper, cut and fold the extra patterns to practice the assembly technique.

INSTRUCTIONS

petal circle in a square box

1. Rough-cut the box lid and base patterns and tape them to the right side of the paper (the outside surface of the box). Cut right through the patterns to cut out the box lid and base.

2. Referring to the patterns, score and crease all the folding lines, making mountain folds on the right side of the paper. Unfold the units completely. Lightly draw diagonal lines from corner to corner on the center square of the lid.

3. Flip both units over to the reverse side (Drawing 1, page 43, bottom) and place pieces of tape to reinforce the areas indicated. Rub and press on the tape to secure it to the paper.

4. Crease folding line A1 (Drawing 2, page 43, bottom), aligning the cut edge of the paper with folding line A2. Rotate the paper ¼ turn to the right and crease folding line B1 so the cut edge aligns with folding line B2. Repeat rotating the piece while folding lines C1 and D1.

5. Raise side A into an upright position to form one side of the box along folding line A2 (Drawing 3, page 43, bottom). Fold and swing down the A tabs to form one corner of the box. Rotate the piece ¼ turn to side B. Lift side B into an upright position, open folding line B1 and fold down side B, overlapping the A tabs. This will lock the corner. Fold and swing down the B tabs to form another corner. Continue to fold all sides and corners as the A side. At the final corner, gently lift up the flap of side A and carefully tuck the D tabs under it.

6. Rough-cut the pattern for the box lid circle. Make tiny pinholes through each dot on the circle edge and at the center. Tape the pattern to the selected paper. Transfer the pinhole dots with a sharp pencil. Cut out the circle. With light pencil lines, connect the edge dots from side to side through the center dot, dividing the circle into eight segments. Glue the circle in place, aligning the pencil lines on the circle with the diagonal lines on the lid.

7. Rough-cut the pattern for the flower. Make many pinholes around the circle line at the center of the flower pattern and tape the pattern to the reverse side of the flower paper. Use a sharp pencil in the pinholes to transfer the center circle. Cut out the flower. Connect the pencil dots to complete the circle and lightly score it. Flip over the flower so the right side of the paper is facing up. Holding the center against the work surface, lift up the flower petals around the scored center circle. Glue only the flower center, on the lid, aligning the crevices of the petals with the pencil lines drawn on the circle. Gently erase.

8. Rough-cut the center circle pattern and make a tiny pinhole in each dot on the circle. Stack and tape together the two small paper squares and tape the pattern on top. Use a pencil to transfer the dots onto the top paper. Cut out the circles and, score the straight lines from dot to dot on one circle. Fold along the score lines to change the circle into a white square with color at the center. Glue the square on the remaining white circle. Glue this unit on the flower.

PETAL CIRCLE IN A SQUARE CARD, PAGE 41

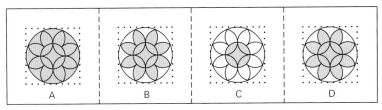

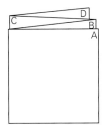

1. Tape four photocopies together to make a pattern for the inside of the unfolded card. Add color to the shaded portions to indicate the cutting area on each panel. The shaded area on Panel D will be cut out of the pattern, but not the card.

2. Accordion-fold the pattern and check for the alignment of the motifs.

3. Reserve the cut-out flower and pattern from Panel D. Cut the flower into four tulip-shaped segments. Glue the segments in place on panel D.

PETAL CIRCLE IN A SQUARE BOX, PAGE 42

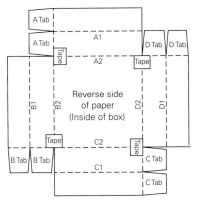

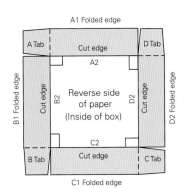

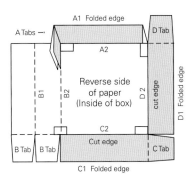

1. On the reverse side of the paper place pieces of tape to reinforce the areas indicated.

2. Crease along folding lines A1, B1, C1, and D1 bringing the cut edges of the paper to meet folding lines A2, B2, C2, and D2.

3. Fold the box sides and corners and overlap the tabs.

AROUND THE WORLD

Cut a single big block or a repeat pattern of four miniature blocks to make an Around the World quilt with duplex paper. To create a quick additional design, save all the pieces cut from each card and glue these little leftovers on a two-panel card or a gift tag, using the cut-out pattern as a template.

MATERIALS

For one 4" (10.2-cm) square card, Design 1 or Design 2 (see note below)

Photocopy of patterns, page 115

Equipment in the Work Box, pages 13–15

4 by 12" (10.2 by 30.5-cm) piece of duplex cardstock

Envelope, 4¼ by 5⅛" (10.8 by 13.0-cm), or Envelope A pattern, page 104, and instructions, pages 103–104

Note: Card Design 2 pattern can be found on page 115.

Top: Card Design 1; Bottom (L to R): Card Design 1, Bonus Card, Gift Tags

INSTRUCTIONS

1. Score, fold, and trim the cardstock to make a three-paneled 4" (10.2-cm) card (Drawing 1). Fold Panel 1 behind Panel 2.

2. Precisely cut out the photocopied pattern of choice, Design 1 or Design 2, on the solid and dotted straight lines without cutting into the curved areas.

3. Place the unfolded cardstock on the work surface so the inside surface of the card is facing up. This is the surface that will eventually show through the cut-out areas on the front of the card.

4. Align the edges and tape the pattern in place on Panel 2 (Drawing 2). Tape the unfolded card to the work surface.

5. Cut out the motif design (including all the curved areas) directly through the pattern and the cardstock. Remove and reserve the pattern and the cut-out pieces of cardstock for the Bonus Card.

6. Remove the card from the work surface. Fold Panel 1 over Panel 2. Close the card so Panel 2 is the card front with Panel 1 behind it. Trim away a narrow strip along the vertical cut edge of Panel 1 if it does not fit well when folded behind Panel 2.

bonus card

1. Follow the previous instructions through Step 5. Tape the reserved pattern to the front of a 4-inch (10.2-cm) single-fold card. Fit the reserved cut-outs from the completed Design 1 or Design 2 card into the openings of the pattern-template and glue them in place on the front of the single-fold card. To make the gift tags, cut the leftover pattern for the Design 2 card into four 2" (5.1-cm) quarter sections. Tape each pattern section to a single-fold 2" (5.1-cm) tag. Glue the reserved cut-out pieces in place. Remove the template promptly so it will not adhere to the card.

1. Score, fold, and trim the card stock, placing Panel 1 behind Panel 2.

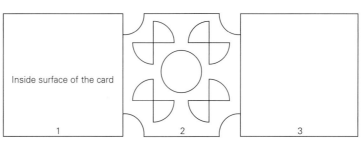

2. Unfold the card and tape the pattern to Panel 2.

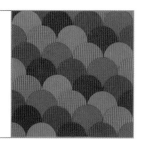

CLAM SHELL

I have read that this early Clam Shell design was a Cape Cod favorite and, because of its very challenging construction, even expert quilters chose to begin the quilt at the center and add patches in all four directions. Here are two ways to interpret the pattern in paper, with scalloped scissors or with a circle punch.

MATERIALS

For one 4¼" (10.8-cm) square card

Photocopy of the card pattern (for Design 1 or Design 2) and the motif base (for Design 1 only), page 112

Equipment in the Work Box, pages 13–15

4¼ by 12¾" (10.8 by 32.4-cm) piece of cardstock

Five 2 by 4" (5.1 by 10.2-cm) pieces of colored paper

Paper punch: ½" (1.3-cm) diameter circle for Design 1 (See note.)

Scalloped-edged scissors, ¼" (6.4-mm) for Design 2

Envelope, 4⅜ by 5¾" (11.1 by 14.6-cm), or Envelope B pattern, page 105, and instructions, pages 103–104

Note: If the punched circles are not precisely ½" (1.3 cm), use a photocopier to adjust the size of the motif base pattern or draw a new one on graph paper. On the card pattern, adjust the size of the Panel 1 window square and the Panel 2 motif placement square accordingly.

(L to R): Card Design 1, Card Design 2

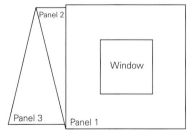

1. Score and accordion-fold the card stock.

INSTRUCTIONS
card design 1

1. Precisely cut out the double-paneled pattern. To complete the pattern, draw and cut an additional 4¼" (10.8-cm) square for Panel 3 and tape it along the top of Panel 2 as shown on pattern page 112. Use a pin to pierce each corner of the large Design 1 window opening square on Panel 1 and the large Design 1 motif base placement square on Panel 2. Put the pattern aside.

2. Score and accordion-fold the cardstock (Drawing 1), then unfold it. Select the surface of the paper preferred for the outside of the card and place it face down on the work surface. Clip or tape the pattern to the cardstock. Mark each pinhole in the pattern with a pencil dot on the cardstock. Remove the pattern. On the card, connect the Panel 1 dots to draw the large square window opening and cut it out. Connect the Panel 2 dots to draw the large square motif base, but do not cut it out. Put the card aside.

3. To make a color key, punch out one circle of each color and line them up horizontally in the preferred sequence. Label the circles 1–5 and tape them in order horizontally on scrap paper. Punch nine circles of color 3 and eight circles of each of the other colors. Cut out the motif base pattern precisely on the outline. Starting at the top of the motif base, glue the first five circles in sequence directly on the pattern. Use just a dot of glue at the bottom of each circle instead of trying to glue the entire surface. The resulting texture will add another dimension to the design and messy glue spots will be avoided.

Overlap the five circles of the first row with four offset circles in the next row. Follow the sequence of colors numbered on the pattern, completely covering the motif base with overlapped circles. Place the motif base in position on Panel 2 and secure it with a piece of removable tape.

4. Fold up Panel 1 so it overlaps Panel 2 with the cut edge at the top (Drawing 1). If the motif aligns with the window in Panel 1 glue the motif in place on Panel 2 and fold and glue Panel 1 over it. Otherwise, make the necessary adjustments, either repositioning the motif or enlarging the window somewhat. Fold down Panel 3 to make the card back.

card design 2

1. To make a miniature version of the motif, use scallop-edged scissors to cut 2½" (6.4-cm) wide rows from narrow strips of colored papers. Draw straight pencil lines on the paper strips and hold the scissors so the crevice edge of the blade just touches the guideline when cutting. For the motif base, draw and cut a 2½" (6.4-cm) square from small-grid graph paper. Starting at the top, glue the first row of scallops in place. Overlap the first row with the second, offsetting the second row so the scallops rest midway between those on the first row. When the motif is finished, refer to Card Design 1, Steps 1 and 2, to prepare the cardstock, but using the smaller 2½" (6.4-cm) Panel 2 motif area on Panel 2 of the pattern. Also use the smaller 1⅝" (4.1-cm) window on Panel 1. To finish, use Step 4 of the instructions for Design 1.

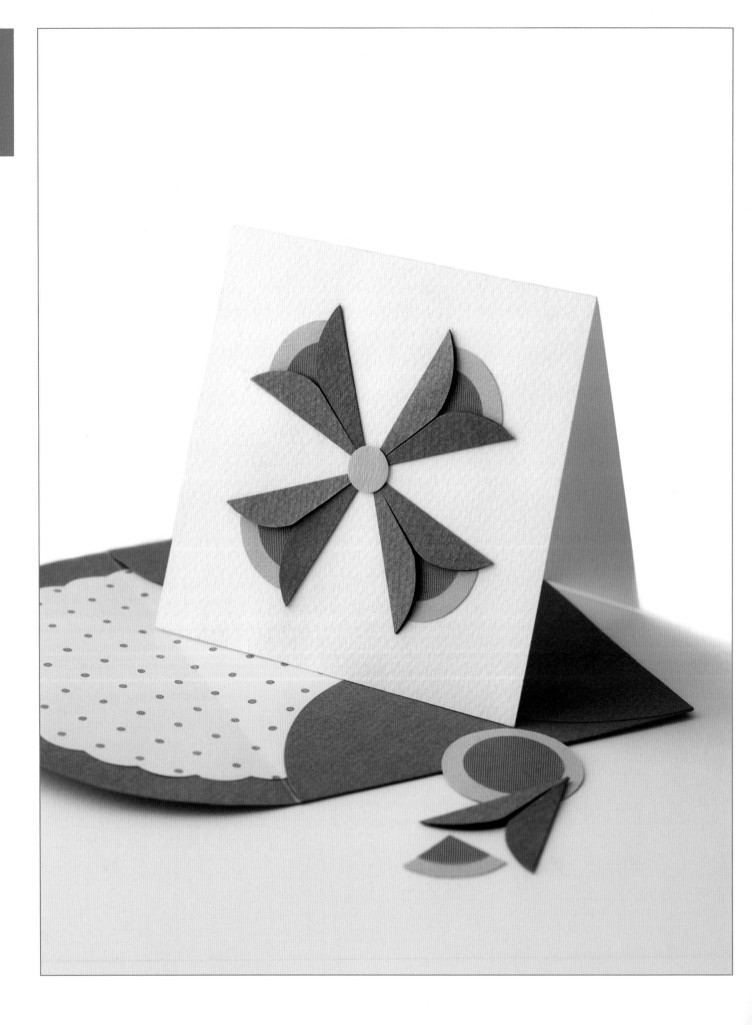

GRANDMA'S TULIPS

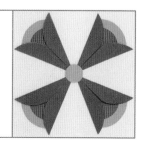

A bunch of pretty tulips brought in from a cottage garden and set on the kitchen table may have inspired this pleasing floral patch. Perhaps, as sometimes was the case, cups and saucers from the kitchen cupboards were used as templates to make the curved pattern pieces for the original block. This design dates back to the early 1930s and the colors of paper used here are very close to those stitched on a Grandma's Tulips quilt from that time.

MATERIALS

For one 4¼" (10.8-cm) square card

Photocopy of the patterns, page 109

Equipment in the Work Box, pages 13–15

4¼ by 8½" (10.8 by 21.6-cm) piece of cardstock, scored and folded to make a 4¼" (10.8-cm) square card

2½ by 6½" (6.4 by 16.5-cm) piece of paper for the leaves

Two 2" (5.1-cm) squares, each a different color, for the tulips

Paper punch: ½" (1.3-cm) circle

Paper scrap for the center circle

Envelope, 4⅜ by 5¾" (11.1 by 14.6-cm), or Envelope B pattern, page 105, and instructions, pages 103–104

Grandma's Tulips Card

INSTRUCTIONS

1. Draw very light pencil lines diagonally across the front of the folded card. Place a dot at the point where the lines intersect at the center and set the card aside.

2. Cut out the card pattern guide precisely on the outline. Also cut out each shaded area to make a template of the pattern guide. Use a pin to pierce the eight circled leaf tips.

3. Tape or clip the pattern guide onto the card front. Use a sharp pencil in each pinhole to transfer the placement of the leaf tips. Also draw within each cut out area to transfer the placement of the center circle and the four tulips. Remove and reserve the pattern guide and put the card aside.

4. Rough-cut the two patterns for the tulip circles and tape one to each colored paper square. First, cut right through the pattern and paper on the crossed lines that divide each circle into quarter sections, then cut on the circle outlines.

Center and glue each smaller circle section on each larger one and allow the pieces to dry. Glue each tulip quarter circle on the card front.

5. Use a craft knife to precisely cut out the copied rectangle that contains the four leaf patterns. Score and fold the leaf paper in half lengthwise with the right side of the paper on the outside. Tape together the cut edge opposite the folded edge to flatten the paper. Align the "place-on-fold" edge of the rectangle pattern with the folded edge of the leaf paper and tape the pattern in place. Cut out the four folded leaf sets.

6. Unfold, score, and refold each leaf piece (Drawings 1–4). Glue each leaf unit on the card front, overlapping a tulip and aligning the pointed base of the leaf with the dot at the card center and the tips of the leaves with the dots made in Step 3. Use the paper punch to cut a circle for the center of the card and glue it in place.

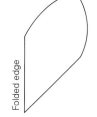

1. Cut out each leaf unit and unfold it.

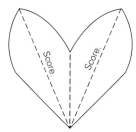

2. On the right side of the paper score each leaf center line from the tip to the point at the base.

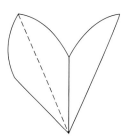

3. Fold one straight leaf edge to the center folding line.

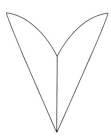

4. Fold the other straight leaf edge to the center folding line.

MOUNTAIN PINK

Just a little sprig of this springtime flower might have inspired the creator of the first Mountain Pink quilt. The pattern for this early 1930s design was advertised and sold mail order by Aunt Martha and Nancy Cabot, two of the many names used for the numerous syndicated columns of the time. Although it looks like appliqué, Mountain Pink is an intricately pieced quilt motif requiring great patience and skill. The paper version of Mountain Pink requires considerable accuracy and attention to detail. It is a good idea to use removable glue here in case the flower and calyx circles need repositioning.

MATERIALS

For one 4¼" (10.8-cm) square card

Three photocopies of the pattern, page 114

Equipment in the Work Box, pages 13–15

4¼ by 12¾" (10.8 by 32.4-cm) piece of cardstock

4" (10.1-cm) square of paper for the flower circle

2½" (6.4-cm) square of paper for the calyx circle

4¼" (10.8-cm) square of paper for the card front, optional

Envelope, 4⅜ by 5¾" (11.1 by 14.6-cm), or Envelope B pattern, page 105, and instructions, pages 103–104

Mountain Pink Card

INSTRUCTIONS

1. To make a complete three panel pattern for the inside surface of the card, precisely cut out the square panel on each copy. Tape the copies together side by side and label them from left to right in ABC order.

2. Refer to the pattern and highlight the proper design area on each panel (Drawing 1). The solid line circle is for Panel A. The dotted line circle is for Panel B. On only Panel B, cut the dotted line circle from the pattern to make a template. The cluster of flowers is for Panel C; do not cut it out at this time. On Panel C, trim the pattern by cutting along the dotted line on the right hand edge.

3. Fold the pattern so that Panel C rests over Panel B and under Panel A (Drawing 2). All the motifs will be inside the folded pattern. Hold it against a bright window to make sure the motifs on each panel align perfectly.

4. On both the front and the back surfaces of the cardstock, measure and draw the folding lines between the three panels. Mark the panels on both sides of the paper with A, B, or C. Each panel should have the same letter on the front and the back.

5. Clip the pattern onto the cardstock, aligning all the edges except the right edge of Panel C. Glue the optional card front paper to the reverse side of Panel A and allow the glue to dry completely. Use a pencil to lightly draw around the inside of the circle template on Panel B to transfer the placement line for the flower circle.

6. Tape the pattern to the cardstock. Using a new knife blade and, cutting right through the pattern and the cardstock, cut out the solid line circle on Panel A. Do not cut Panel B at all. On Panel C, carefully and slowly cut out the cluster of flowers. Whenever possible, cut toward the center of the cluster to maintain the sharp points and crevices of the petals. Trim the edge of the Panel C cardstock to match the trimmed pattern edge. On the reverse side of the card, lightly score the two penciled folding lines between the three panels. Set the card aside.

7. Rough-cut the patterns for the flower circle and the calyx circle. Cut out the small circle at the center of the large flower circle pattern. Tape each pattern to its proper paper. Use a pencil to draw the small placement line circle in the center of the large circle. Cut out each circle, but do not cut out the center penciled circle on the largest one. Glue the calyx circle within the placement area drawn at the center of the large circle. Glue the flower circle within the placement area drawn on Panel B.

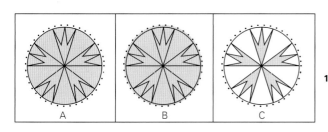

1. Make a complete pattern for the inside of the card. Highlight and label each panel: A, B, or C.

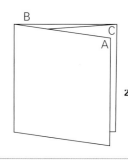

2. Fold the pattern with Panel C over Panel B, and under Panel A.

4

RISING STARS

Nature was always the primary source of ideas for quilt motifs. Stars in the night sky, symbols of faith and hope, inspired an entire universe of patchwork patterns. Star blocks, too many to count, far outnumber all other quilt designs, suggesting that the star has long been the quilter's favorite motif.

Star of Bethlehem (page 56)

RISING STARS

Rising Stars, also known as Stars and Squares, was the inspiration for an endless variety of simple and elaborate designs in the patchwork galaxy. In 1929, author Ruth Finley had something to say about this motif in the pages of *Old Patchwork Quilts and the Women Who Made Them,* a primer on quilt lore and history. She praised the design as an "ancient pattern" and a "great star favorite."

MATERIALS

For one 4¼" (10.8-cm) square card

Photocopy of the patterns, page 114

Equipment in the Work Box, pages 13–15

4¼ by 8½" (10.8 by 21.6-cm) piece of cardstock, scored and folded to make a 4¼" (10.8-cm) square card

4" (10.2-cm) square piece of paper for the background

4¼" (10.8-cm) square of paper for the big star

2" (5.1-cm) square of paper for the large star center

2¼" (5.7-cm) square of paper for the small star

1" (2.5-cm) square of paper for the small star center

Envelope, 4⅜ by 5¾" (11.1 by 14.6-cm), or Envelope B pattern, page 105, and instructions, pages 103–104

Rising Stars Cards

INSTRUCTIONS

1. Rough-cut both star patterns close to the edges. Tape each pattern to the paper of choice and cut out one of each star. Set the pieces aside.

2. In the order suggested, center and glue each motif on the next. Start with the smallest square and glue it at the center of the small star. Glue the star unit to the medium square and then glue the large star behind it. After placing the large star on the largest square, glue the motif on the card.

STAR OF BETHLEHEM

The format of a Star of Bethlehem quilt is most often one huge central star that creates a wonderful radiating pattern of illusion. Depending on the placement of the dark and light diamond-shaped patches that create the motif, the design is known by several other names including Lone Star, Prairie Star, Virginia Star, Stars of Alabama, Sunburst Star, Morning Star, Star Bouquet, and Star of Hope. An ornament or a gift tag can be made from the leftover shapes cut from each panel of the card. Simply stack and stick the pieces together with glue or foam tape. Then punch a hole in one star point and add a string tie.

MATERIALS

For one 4¼" (10.8-cm) square card, Design 1 or Design 2

Three photocopies of the pattern, page 120

Equipment in the Work Box, pages 13–15

4¼ by 17" (approximately 10.8 by 43.2-cm) piece of duplex paper

Envelope, 4⅜ by 5¾" (11.1 by 14.6-cm), or Envelope B pattern, page 105, and instructions, pages 103–104

Top: Card Design 1; Bottom: Gift Tag or Ornament, Card Design 2, Card Design 1

INSTRUCTIONS

design 1

1. To make the card pattern, precisely cut the 4¼" (10.8-cm) square from each of the photocopies. Label the copies A, B, and C. For Panel D, cut an additional 4¼" (10.8-cm) square from scrap paper. Tape the identical copies together, side-by-side, in ABC order (Drawing 1). Tape Panel D to Panel C. This is the pattern for the inside surface of the unfolded card. To indicate the cutting area on each panel, use a pencil or a marker to add color to the shaded areas on Drawing 2.

2. Accordion-fold the pattern into the square format (Drawing 3). All the design motifs will be inside the pattern.

Hold the pattern against a sunny window to check the alignment of the card edges and the design motifs on each panel. Adjust if necessary. Lightly score and accordion-fold the duplex paper into the card format (Drawing 3). Place the unfolded card on the work surface so the inside surface of the card faces up. Discreetly label the panels from left to right in ABCD order.

3. Tape the unfolded card onto the work surface and tape the pattern on top of it. Cutting directly through the pattern and the card paper, cut out the shaded design areas on Panels A, B, and C. Remove the pattern and refold the card.

design 2

1. In addition to the materials listed for Card Design 1, you will need a 3¾" (9.5-cm) square of white paper for Design 2. Complete Steps 1 and 2 for Design 1. Before starting Step 3, center and glue the square of white paper behind Panel C. Although it will seem counter-intuitive, the white square is actually being correctly placed on the outside surface of the card. Complete Step 3 for Design 1.

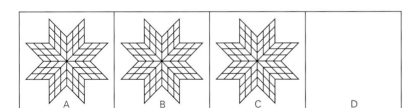

1. Tape the photocopies and one additional square together to make a pattern for the inside of the unfolded card.

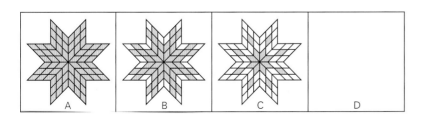

2. Add color to the shaded portions to indicate the cutting area on each panel.

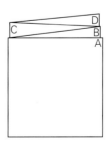

3. Accordion-fold the pattern and check for the alignment of the motifs.

CIRCLE STAR

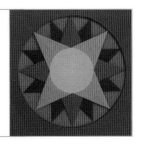

Four paper squares, clipped and folded to make individual four-pointed stars, are stacked, glued, and topped with a circle to create the pattern known as Circle Star. Use the same folding technique and add a backing to make Four-Pointed Star ornament.

MATERIALS

card

For one 4¼" (10.8-cm) square card

Equipment in the Work Box, pages 13–15

4¼ by 8½" (10.8 by 21.6-cm) piece of cardstock, scored and folded to make 4¼" (10.8-cm) square card

Four 2¼" (5.7-cm) squares of origami or text paper for the star units; 1 yellow-orange, 1 orange, 2 red

1⁵⁄₁₆" (3.3-cm) diameter circle of paper for the center

4¼" (10.8-cm) square of contrasting paper for inside the card

Foam layering tape, optional

Envelope, 4⅜ by 5¾" (11.1 by 14.6-cm), or Envelope B pattern, page 105, and instructions, pages 102–104

ornament

For one 4½" (11.4-cm) diameter star

Photocopy of the base pattern, page 115

Two 3½" (8.9-cm) squares of paper

10" (25.4-cm) length of monofilament

INSTRUCTIONS

card

1. No patterns are needed. Place the star papers right side up on the work surface. Make the four star units (Drawings 1–6). Unfold the paper before making each new fold. Turn the stars over so the right side of the paper is facing up.

2. Start at the top and align the crevices of each star with the folding lines of the one below it. Stack, rotate, and glue the units together to make a sixteen-point star with two red stars at the bottom of the stack. Glue the center circle on top. Set the star aside.

3. On the reverse side of the card front, draw diagonal lines to mark the center point. On this surface, center, draw, and cut out a circle approximately 3" (7.6-cm) in diameter.

4. Glue the remaining 4¼" (10.8-cm) paper square on the inside of the card back so the new color shows through the front cut-out circle.

Draw light diagonal lines on this surface. Using the lines for guidance, position the star on the inside of the card. Each point of the top star unit should touch one of the diagonal lines. Place foam tape or glue on the reverse side of the star and attach it to the inside of the card within the circle opening.

ornament

1. Fold the front of the star (Drawings 1–6), but do not turn the completed unit over to the right side. Work on the reverse side to give the star dimension, overlapping the folded flaps of each point. Glue the overlapped flaps together, sandwiching the cut ends of the looped monofilament between the flaps on one point.

2. Rough-cut the pattern for the base and tape it to the remaining square. Cut out the shape through the pattern and paper, and glue it to the reverse side of the star using quick-drying glue. Trim away any excess.

Top: Four-Pointed Star Ornaments;
Bottom: Circle Star Card

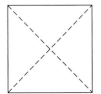

1. Place the paper right side up on the work surface and make diagonal mountain folds across it.

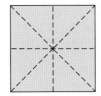

2. Make horizontal and vertical valley folds. Turn the square to the reverse side.

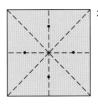

3. Make dots to mark the cutting lines on the horizontal and vertical folding lines, ½" (1.3-cm) from each edge of a 2¼" (5.7-cm) card square and ¾" (1.9-cm) from each edge of a 3½" (8.9-cm) ornament square.

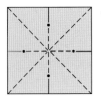

4. Make slots around the square cutting from each edge of the paper to the nearby dot on the horizontal and vertical folding lines.

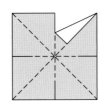

5. Make the first point of the star, folding one edge of the paper to meet the diagonal folding line.

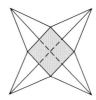

6. Fold the remaining points of the star and turn the unit over to the right side.

GLITTERING STAR

One of the many descendants of the Rising Star dynasty, Glittering Star is also known as the Morning Star. Two variations on this design are offered here, a four-panel card and an easier two-panel multiprint version.

MATERIALS

For one 4¼" (10.8-cm) square card, Design 1

For Design 2, see note below

Three photocopies of the pattern, page 113

Equipment in the Work Box, pages 13–15

4¼ by 17" (approximately 10.8 by 43.2-cm) piece of lightweight duplex paper

Pinking shears, optional

Envelope, 4⅜ by 5¾" (11.1 by 14.6-cm), or Envelope B pattern, page 105, and instructions, pages 103–104

Note: Card Design 2 requires only one pattern copy, a single-fold 4¼" (10.8-cm) square card, and six 1½" (3.8-cm) squares of paper.

Top: Card Design 2; Bottom: (L and R) Card Design 1

INSTRUCTIONS

design 1

1. To make the card pattern, precisely cut the 4¼" (10.8-cm) square from each of the three copies. Label the copies A, B, and C. For Panel D, cut an additional 4¼" (10.8-cm) square from scrap paper. Tape the three identical copies together, side-by-side, in ABC order and tape Panel D to Panel C (Drawing 1). This is the pattern for the inside of the unfolded card. To indicate the cutting areas, use a pencil or a marker to add color to the shaded portions of the pattern.

2. Accordion-fold the pattern into a 4¼" (10.8-cm) format (Drawing 2). All the design motifs will be inside the pattern. Hold the pattern against a sunny window to check the alignment of the card edges and the design motifs. Adjust if necessary.

3. Lightly score and accordion-fold the duplex paper and unfold it. Tape the paper on the work surface so the inside surface of the card (blue in the photo) is facing up and tape the pattern on top. Cutting directly through the pattern and the card paper, cut out the shaded design areas on Panels A, B, and C. Remove the pattern and refold the card.

4. To add a zigzag border, first make a ¼" (6.4-mm) frame for the front of the card by cutting a 3¾" (9.5-cm) square from the center of an additional 4¼" (10.8-cm) square. Also cut two ½ by 4" (1.3 by 10.2-cm) strips of paper and make a pencil line through the center for the entire length of each strip. Use pinking shears to cut along the center line, dividing each strip into two pieces. While cutting, hold the shears in such a way so that either the crevices or the points along the blades just touch the pencil guideline. Center and glue the strips on the reverse side of the frame around the inner edges and glue the frame to the card.

5. To enclose the star block within a very narrow frame, carefully cut a 3" (7.6-cm) square from a 3⅛" (7.9-cm) square and glue the fragile frame in place on the card front.

design 2

1. Rough-cut three individual stars from a single photocopy of the pattern. Stack and tape together three layers of three different print papers. Tape a single star pattern to the top of each stack. Cutting directly through the pattern, cut each stack to make a total of nine stars. Arrange and glue the stars in a pleasing order on a 3" (7.6-cm) square of paper. Center and glue the star square on a 3¼" (8.3-cm) border square if desired and then glue the unit on a single-fold card.

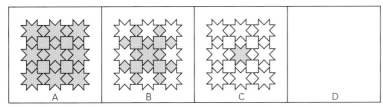

1. Tape three photocopies and one additional square together to make a pattern for the inside of the unfolded card. Add color to the shaded portions to indicate the cutting area on each panel.

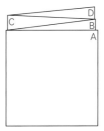

2. Accordion-fold the pattern to check the alignment.

STAR OF SWEDEN

The discovery of the Star of Sweden was made in Augusta, Maine. Readers of *Comfort*, a magazine published there from 1888–1942, were the first to mail order the design from the many patterns offered. The original Star of Sweden block held a single octagonal star. For greater interest, three concentric stars shine together on this four-paneled card.

MATERIALS

card

For one 4" (10.2-cm) square card

Photocopies of the three patterns, pages 116–117

Equipment in the Work Box, pages 13–15

4 by 16" (approximately 10.2 by 40.6-cm) piece of lightweight duplex paper

Envelope, 4¼ by 5⅛" (10.8 by 13.0-cm), or Envelope A pattern, page 104, and instructions, pages 103–104

Top: Star of Sweden Basket with Handle; Bottom (L to R): Star of Sweden Card, Star of Sweden Basket

INSTRUCTIONS

card

1. Precisely cut patterns for Panels A, B, and C. From scrap paper, cut an additional 4" (10.1-cm) square for Panel D. Tape the patterns side by side in reverse DCBA order (Drawing 1). Accordion-fold the pattern (Drawing 2) and hold it against a bright window to check the alignment of the card edges and the motifs on each panel. Adjust if necessary.

2. Tape the card paper onto the work surface so the outside color of the card (white in the photo) faces up. With Panel A on the right, tape the pattern on top of the card paper. On Panel A, use a very fine pin to pierce the eight end points (circled on the pattern) of the intersecting cutting lines that form a star motif. Still working on Panel A, pierce the eight points around the square panel where each tip of the dotted star outline touches the edge of the card.

3. Cut the solid intersecting lines of the motif on Panel A cutting directly through the pattern and the card paper as though slicing a pie into eight equal sections. Refer to the circled points on the remaining patterns and Step 2, above, to prepare Panels B and C and cut the pie slices on each panel. Make a few pinholes to

transfer the vertical folding lines between the panels. Remove the pattern. On each panel, if the pie-slice cuts do not meet the pinholes made in Step 2, extend the cutting lines until they do.

4. Note the folding lines that form an octagon at the center of Panels A, B, and C on the pattern. Score these folding lines from pinhole to pinhole as follows. On Panels A and C, score the lines on the yellow side (inside) of the card. On Panel B, score on the white side (outside) of the card.

5. Score the vertical folding lines between the panels by connecting the pinholes. Score the lines between Panels A and B and Panels C and D on the white side (outside) of the card. Score the line between Panels B and C on the inside. Fold the card as in Drawing 2.

6. Lift up each star point at the center of Panel A and fold it back and down onto the card front (Drawing 3). The tip of each folded star point should touch one of the eight pinholes (see Step 2). Keeping the card folded and working through the open area at the center of the motif, fold each star point on Panel B (Drawing 4, page 64), then on Panel C (Drawing 5, page 64).

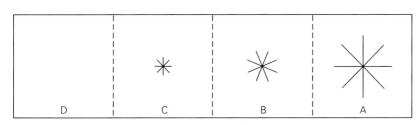

1. Tape the pattern panels together in reverse order: D C B A.

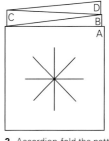

2. Accordion-fold the pattern to check the alignment.

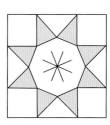

3. Fold the star points on Panel A.

STAR OF SWEDEN

MATERIALS

basket

For one 1¹⁄₁₆ by 2⅛" (2.7 by 5.4-cm) basket, interior space

Photocopy of both basket patterns, pages 116–117

Equipment in the Work Box, pages 13–15

2¾ by 8" (7.0 by 20.3-cm) piece of paper for the basket side and star points

5" (12.7-cm) square of paper for the base

⅜ by 6" (9.5mm by 15.2-cm) piece of paper for the handle, optional

INSTRUCTIONS

basket

1. Rough-cut the basket side pattern and tape it to the proper paper. If using duplex paper, the star point color should be facing up. Referring to the top edge of the pattern, use a pin to pierce each dot that rests on the horizontal folding line along the base of the star points. Also pierce the dots along the lower straight edge of the pattern, placing one pinhole at each vertical folding line.

2. Cut right through the pattern and the paper to make one basket side piece. On the top edge, score the horizontal folding line along the base of the star points. Turn the piece to the reverse side and score each short vertical line from the crevice at the top edge to the pinhole near the lower edge.

Curl the piece into a ring, glue the side tab in place outside the basket, and set it aside.

3. Rough-cut the base pattern and tape it to the paper of choice. The color for the interior base of the basket should be facing down. Cut directly through the pattern and paper. To make the base folding lines, score the star shape from one crevice to the next to create a faint hexagon on the base. Join the base and the basket side piece folding up the base star points and gluing them outside the basket. Match the tip of each base star point with one of the pinholes made on the folding line at the top edge of the basket side piece. Fold down the star points around the top edge of the basket so they are parallel to the work surface. Glue the ends of the optional handle inside the basket.

card drawings, continued

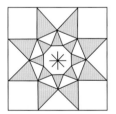

4. Fold the star points on Card Panel B.

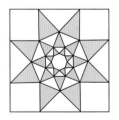

5. Fold the star points on Card Panel C.

Card Tricks: Stars and Planets

This charming motif is reminiscent of the cartoonlike "Outer Space" drawings of the 1930s and '40s. The card is quickly made by stacking and gluing the two planet layers together then adding a star at the center of the universe to complete the design.

MATERIALS

For one 4¼" (10.8-cm) square card

Photocopy of the patterns, page 113

Equipment in the Work Box, pages 13–15

4¼ by 8½" (10.8 by 21.6-cm) piece of cardstock, scored and folded to make a 4¼" (10.8-cm) square card

Two different 2¾" (7.0-cm) squares of paper for the large and small planets

3¾" (9.5-cm) square of paper for the star

Foam tape, optional

Envelope, 4⅜ by 5¾" (11.1 by 14.6-cm) or Envelope B pattern, page 105, and instructions, pages 103–104

Note: To make the card with a border, center and glue the motif on a 4" (10.2-cm) square of paper and then center and glue the square on the card.

INSTRUCTIONS

1. Rough-cut the three patterns close to the outlines. Tape each pattern to the paper of choice. Before cutting Planet Layer 1, transfer the dots by piercing the pattern and paper with a pin. Cut right through the patterns to make the planets and stars and set the pieces aside.

2. In the order suggested, center and glue each motif on the next. Place Planet Layer 1 on the work surface and add a small amount of glue at the center. Place Planet Layer 2 on top of it. Match the crevices of scalloped Layer 2 with the pinholes on Planet Layer 1. Align the points of the star layer with the crevices on Planet Layer 2 and glue the pieces together. Center and glue the motif on the extra square noted after the material list or center and glue the motif directly on the card. To add dimension, attach the motif with pieces of foam tape instead of glue.

STAR OF CHAMBLIE

Carrie Hall, in her 1933 classic, *The Romance of the Patchwork Quilt in America,* describes the Star of Chamblie: "An antique design brought to Canada from France in the early part of the nineteenth century." The red, green, and chrome yellow used for this paper portrait of the motif are very close to a 1930s sample block from a collection in the Spenser Museum of Art at the University of Kansas in Lawrence, Kansas.

MATERIALS

For one 4¼" (10.8-cm) card

Three photocopies of the pattern, page 118

Equipment in the Work Box, pages 13–15

4¼ by 17" (approximately 10.8 by 43.2-cm) piece of white cardstock

Two 4" (10.2-cm) squares of coordinating text-weight paper (red and green in the photo)

Eight ¼" (6.4-mm) squares of coordinating paper (yellow in the photo)

Envelope, 4⅜ by 5¾" (11.1 by 14.6-cm), or Envelope B pattern, page 105, and instructions, pages 103–104

Star of Chamblie Card

INSTRUCTIONS

1. To make the card pattern, precisely cut the 4¼" (10.8-cm) square from each of the three photocopies. Label the copies A, B, and C. For Panel D, cut an additional 4¼" (10.8-cm) square from scrap paper. Tape the three identical copies together, side by side, in ABC order (Drawing 1). Tape Panel D to Panel C. This is the pattern for the inside of the unfolded card. To indicate the cutting area on each panel of the pattern, use a pencil or a marker to add color to the shaded areas on Drawing 2.

2. Accordion-fold the pattern into the 4¼" (10.8-cm) format shown on Drawing 3. All the design motifs will be inside the pattern. Hold the pattern against a sunny window to check the alignment of the card edges and the design motifs on each panel. Adjust if necessary.

3. Lightly score and accordion-fold the cardstock (Drawing 3). Unfold it and place it on the work surface with Panel A on the left. Glue one of the 4" (10.2-cm) squares of paper on Panel B (red in the photo). Glue the remaining 4" (10.2-cm) square on the reverse side of Panel C (yellow in the photo).

4. Tape the unfolded card onto the work surface with Panel A to the left. The red square on Panel B will be visible, but the green square on the reverse of Panel C will not. Tape the pattern on the card. Cutting directly through the pattern and cardstock, cut out the shaded design areas on Panels A, B, and C. Remove the pattern and refold the card. Glue the tiny squares in place around the star as shown on Drawing 4.

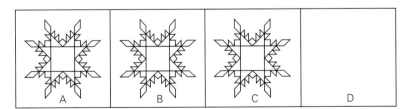

1. Tape three photocopies and one additional square together to make a pattern for the inside of the unfolded card.

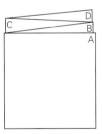

3. Accordion-fold the pattern and check for the alignment of the motifs.

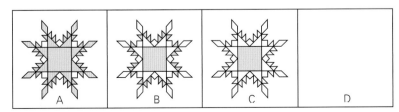

2. Add color to the shaded portions to indicate the cutting area on each panel.

4. Glue the tiny squares around the star.

BLAZING SUN

The combination of the intense orange color and the checkerboard sashing of this Blazing Sun design evokes the sound of cicadas in late August when a burning sun almost shimmers in the sky. The original fabric version of this particular quilt was made in Iowa around 1910, and it is now at home in the collection of the Yakima Valley Museum and Historical Association in Washington state.

MATERIALS

For one 4¼" (10.8-cm) card

Photocopy of the pattern, page 118

Equipment in the Work Box, pages 13–15

4¼ by 8½" (10.8 by 21.6-cm) piece of white cardstock, scored and folded to make a 4¼" (10.8-cm) square card

4½" (11.4-cm) square of orange paper

4½" (11.4-cm) square of green paper

Envelope, 4⅜ by 5¾" (11.1 by 14.6-cm), or Envelope B pattern, page 105, and instructions, pages 103–104

Blazing Sun Card

INSTRUCTIONS

1. Stack and tape together the two squares of colored paper. Rough-cut the photocopied pattern and tape it to the top of the paper stack. Cut right through the pattern and the papers on every solid line to make the paper patches for the card. Reserve the center square pattern that has the sun cut from it, keeping it in the same position in which it was placed on the original full pattern.

2. On the front panel of the card, lightly draw diagonal lines from corner to corner across the square. Using the pencil lines for guidance, center the reserved square pattern on the card, placing it exactly as it was placed on the original pattern. Each corner of the pattern should touch a diagonal line. Adhere the pattern to the card by placing removable tape on two opposite edges. Holding a ruler against each edge of the square pattern, lightly draw horizontal and vertical pencil guidelines extending from each corner of the pattern to each edge of the card. The guidelines will create a square at each corner of the card.

3. Using the taped-on pattern as a template, lift the orange sun from the stack of cut pieces, keeping it in the same position. Fit the sun within the cut opening and glue it in place on the card. Leaving the pattern in place, glue (flush with the two untaped edges of the pattern) two green bars from the stack of pieces in place on the card.

4. Remove the two pieces of tape from the pattern, but do not remove the pattern. Tape the two pattern edges not previously taped. Glue one green bar along each untaped edge. Remove the pattern. Glue the four remaining green bars in place. One long edge of each bar should be flush with an edge of the card and the short edges of each bar should align with the pencil guidelines drawn on each corner of the card in Step 2.

5. To divide the square corners and create checkerboard patterns within them, hold a ruler against each edge of the bars and use a pencil to lightly draw horizontal and vertical guidelines that extend from the ends of every bar to the edges of the paper. Referring to the photo glue small orange squares on each corner of the card in checkerboard fashion.

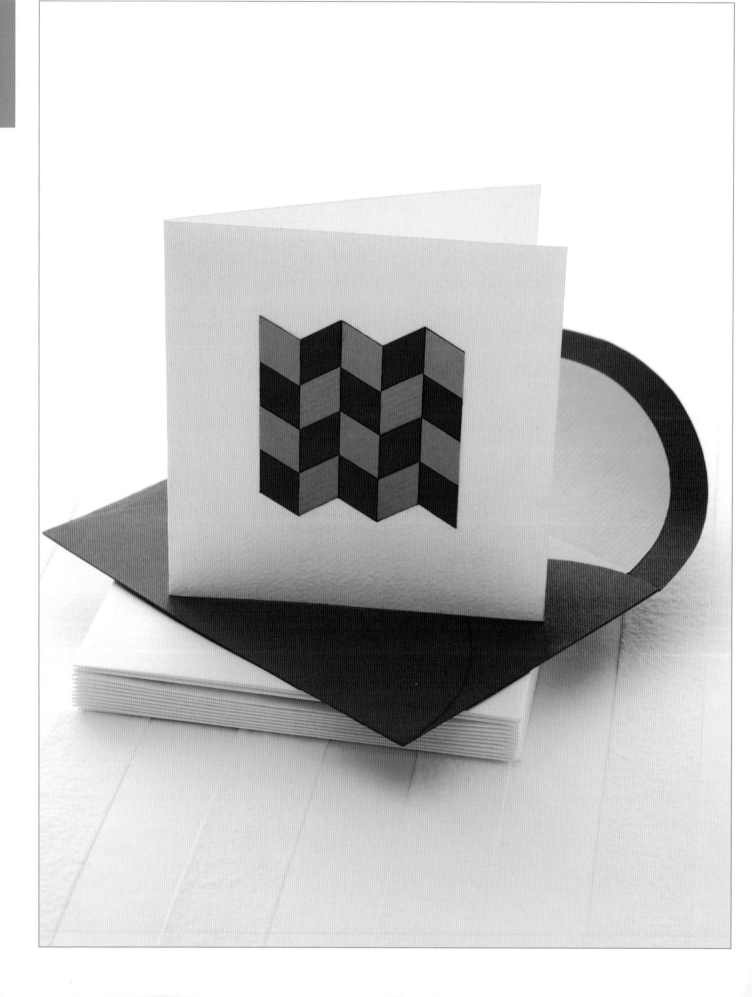

5

THOUSANDS OF TRIANGLES AND DIAMONDS GALORE

One diagonal cut across a square patch divides it into two 45-degree right triangles, each triangle having two equal edges. The zigzag borders of some of the earliest quilts were made by alternately placing light- and dark-colored right triangles together or by combining right triangles with squares. Placing two 60-degree equilateral triangles together creates the diamond patch, one of the favorite but most challenging patterns for quilters.

Rail Fence Card (page 84)

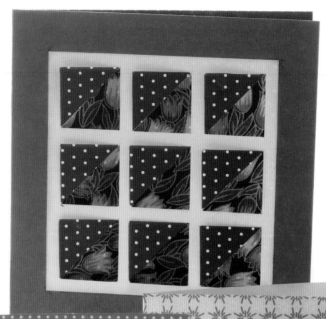

THOUSANDS OF TRIANGLES

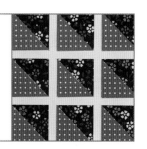

Sometimes the simplest of projects are the most satisfying, especially when the work can be completed in a flash! Thousands of Triangles is just such a design. Plain or patterned duplex scrapbooking paper is perfect for the card since the weight of heavy cardstock impedes the folding and flattening of the triangles on the card front. Making Thousands of Triangles is not only quick and easy, it's also a great way to showcase a favorite piece of paper, inside the card, without cutting it into little pieces.

MATERIALS

For one 4½" (11.4-cm) square card, Design 1 or Design 2

Photocopy of the pattern, page 120

Equipment in the Work Box, pages 13–15

4½ by 9" (11.4 by 22.9-cm) piece of duplex scrapbooking paper, scored and folded to make a 4½" (11.4-cm) square card

4" (10.2-cm) square of decorative paper

4½" (11.4-cm) square of paper for the border, optional

Envelope, 4⅝ by 6⅛" (11.8 by 15.6-cm), or Envelope C pattern, page 105, and instructions, pages 103–104

Top: Card Design 2; Bottom (L to R): Card Design 1, Card Design 2

INSTRUCTIONS

1. Cut out the photocopied pattern precisely on the outline. Use a pin to pierce tiny holes in the pattern at the corner and ends of each angled cutting line circled on the pattern.

2. The interior of the card will provide one of the triangle colors on the outside of the card. Unfold the card and place this preferred triangle color right side up on the work surface. The triangles for Design 1 fold down revealing their interior color. For Design 1, place the pattern using Drawing 1, noting that the star symbol is at the top. The triangles for Design 2 fold up. Place the pattern for Design 2, using Drawing 2, noting that the star symbol on the pattern is on the left side.

3. Tape the pattern to the left panel on the inside of the card. Use a pencil to transfer the position of the pinholes. Cut the angled lines right through the pattern and paper. Remove the pattern. Each cutting line should touch a pencil dot. Adjust if necessary. Lightly score each diagonal folding line.

4. Center and glue the 4" (10.2-cm) square of decorative paper inside the card on the right panel. Close the card and fold out and flatten the triangles. To add the optional border, cut a 3⅜" (8.6-cm) square from the center of the remaining piece of paper. Center and glue the border on the card front.

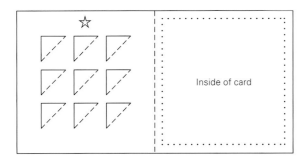

1. Place the pattern in this position inside the card for Design 1.

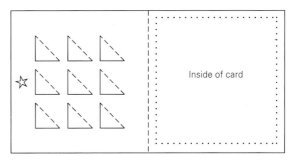

2. Place the pattern in this position inside the card for Design 2.

DIAMONDS GALORE

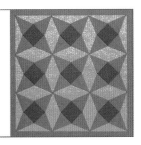

Alternating the color and value of the patches transforms the Diamonds Galore pattern into an Amethyst, a Kaleidoscope, a Wandering Flower, or a Windmill Star. These are just a few of the many imaginative names given to this beguiling old pattern of illusion. A precisely pieced combination of small squares, diamonds, and triangles creates the impression of overlapping circles on a patchwork quilt of this design. Worked in paper, the motifs are simply individual squares, cut and folded to form a collection of four-point stars that are glued to a background square, but the effect is similarly intriguing.

MATERIALS

For one 4½" (11.4-cm) square card

Photocopies of the patterns, page 122

Equipment in the Work Box, pages 13–15

4½" (11.4-cm) square of origami paper for the stars

4¼" (10.8-cm) square of paper for the background

4⅛" (10.5-cm) additional square of paper for a double border on the card, optional

2" (5.1-cm) square of paper for the center of the stars

Envelope C pattern, page 105, and instructions, pages 103–104

Diamonds Galore Card

INSTRUCTIONS

1. To indicate the placement of the stars on the background square, rough-cut the entire large pattern for the nine star squares and tape it to the background paper. The background square of paper is extra-large to allow for adjustments and it will be trimmed later, so do not cut it now. Use a fine pin to precisely pierce the circled tip of each star point on the background square (Drawing 1), passing the pin through both the pattern and the paper. Remove and reserve the pattern and set the background paper aside.

2. Tape the same large pattern onto the star paper and make nine individual square star units by cutting right through the pattern and the paper. Set the nine squares aside.

3. Rough-cut the small pattern for the star centers and tape the pattern in place on the star center paper. Cut right through the pattern and the paper to make nine star centers and put them aside too.

4. Place one star square right side down on the work surface and fold the nine star units (Drawings 2–4). For the greatest accuracy, unfold the paper before making each new fold. Turn the stars over so the smooth side of the paper is facing up.

5. Arrange and glue the stars in place on the background square so each point of each star touches a pinhole. When the glue is dry, carefully trim away the extra background paper to make a square. Center and glue the background on the optional border paper or glue it directly onto the card. Refer to the photo and glue the star centers in place.

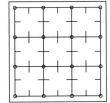

1. Use a pin to mark the placement of the stars on the background square.

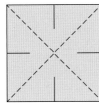

2. Place the star square right side down on the work surface and fold it diagonally in each direction.

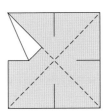

3. Start to make the first point of the star, folding one edge of the paper to meet a diagonal folding line, as shown.

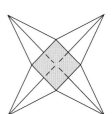

4. Fold the remaining points of the star. Turn the unit over to the right side.

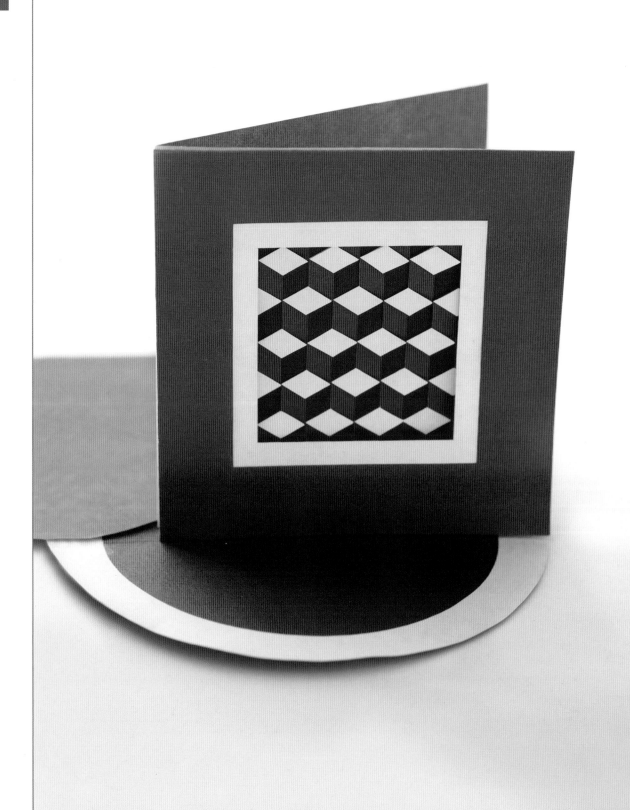

TUMBLING BLOCKS

A few cuts and folds on a piece of duplex paper produce this intriguing pattern of illusion called Tumbling Blocks, Variegated Diamonds, Jacob's Ladder, Steps to the Altar, and quite a few other names. The dimensional impression of the motif is intensified when two dazzling colors are used together with white on the reverse side of the darkest paper. You can glue the white tabs that form the tops of the blocks in place, but it is more fun to leave them unglued so the recipient can lift the tabs. Precise cutting and folding guarantee the best results, so even though this is not the most challenging project in the book, it is definitely not for the faint hearted!

MATERIALS

For one 4" (10.2-cm) square card

Two photocopies of the pattern, page 119

Equipment in the Work Box, pages 13–15

4 by 16" (10.2 by 40.8-cm) piece of dark-colored text-weight paper, reversing to white

3" (7.6-cm) square of medium-colored paper

4" (10.2-cm) square of paper, for a border, optional

Envelope 4¼ by 5⅛" (10.8 by 13.0-cm), or Envelope A pattern, page 104, and instructions, pages 103–104

Tumbling Blocks Card

INSTRUCTIONS

1. Cut out both rectangular patterns on the outlines. Fold one pattern on the folding line and flip it to the reverse (blank) side. Tape the two pattern units together (Drawing 1). The panels are numbered in reverse order. Panels 3 and 4 are blank and no cuts will be made on them. Mark the panel folding lines with a few pin holes. To minimize confusion when cutting Panel 2, use a pin to pierce each point of every diamond in the pattern.

2. Tape the card paper, white side up, onto the work surface. Tape the completed pattern on top of the card. Use a sharp pencil to transfer the pinholes from the pattern to the paper.

3. Using a craft knife and straight edge and cutting right through the pattern, cut out the square on Panel 1. On Panel 2, cut each tab on the solid lines. Remove only the pattern from the work surface. If the cutting lines do not meet the pencil dots made in Step 2, use the knife to extend the lines.

4. Score the folding lines between the panels of the card. Score the broken folding line on each tab. Be sure that the vertical cutting lines on each tab extend down to meet the corresponding folding lines. On Panel 3, center and glue the square of colored paper.

5. Remove the card from the work surface. With the white side of the paper still facing up, push each tab out toward the colored side of the paper, sharply creasing the tab on the folding line.

6. Flip over the card to the colored side. Accordion-fold the card with the white Panel 1 on top (Drawing 2). If a border is desired, cut a 2½" (6.4-cm) square opening in the remaining 4" (10.2-cm) square of paper and glue it in place on the card front.

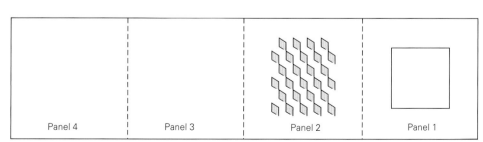

1. Prepare the complete pattern.

Panel 4   Panel 3   Panel 2   Panel 1

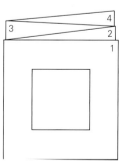

2. Accordion-fold the card.

INDIAN TRAIL

The geographic location of the Indian Trail quiltmaker determined the name of this triangle patchwork. Changing identities from place to place and time to time, the pattern was known as Irish Puzzle, Rambling Road, Winding Walk, Forest Path, Climbing Rose, Prickly Pear, North Wind, Weather Vane, Storm at Sea, Bear's Paw, and Kansas Troubles.

MATERIALS

For one 4½" (11.4-cm) square card

Photocopy of the patterns, page 119

Equipment in the Work Box, pages 13–15

4½ by 9" (11.4 by 22.9-cm) piece of cardstock, scored and folded to make a 4½" (11.4-cm) square card

Three 3½" (8.9-cm) squares of duplex origami paper

3½" (8.9-cm) square of paper for the motif border

Envelope C pattern, page 105, and instructions, pages 103–104

Indian Trail Card

INSTRUCTIONS

1. Draw light diagonal pencil lines across the card front and set the card aside. Rough-cut each pattern.

2. Select the color side of the origami paper preferred for the triangles around the outside edge of the block, (tan in the photo). With this color side up, place one of the duplex paper squares on the work surface. Tape the rough-cut motif square pattern on top of it (Drawing 1). Slice right through the pattern and paper, cutting all the solid cutting lines within the square. Then cut out the motif square itself, keeping it in the same position.

3. Using all the previously cut lines for guidance, draw a grid with light pencil lines on the motif square (Drawing 2). The grid will optimize the accuracy of the folding. Fold over all the little triangles within and around the square (Drawing 3).

4. With the same (tan) color side facing up, place another duplex paper square on the work surface. Tape the rough-cut pattern for the four folded triangles on top of it Cut out the four squares and fold them into triangles so the alternate color of the duplex paper (dark print in the photo) is on the outside. Refer again to the photo and glue the triangles in place on the motif that was cut and folded in Steps 2 and 3.

5. Place the remaining origami square on the work surface so the color facing up is the same that faced up in Step 1. Center and glue the motif on this background square and trim the edges of the square to match the edges of the motif.

6. Center and glue the motif on the border square and then center and glue the border on the card.

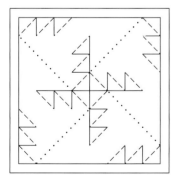

1. Tape the motif pattern to one duplex paper square and cut it out.

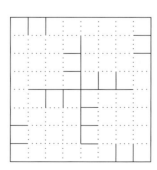

2. Draw a grid of light pencil lines on the motif square.

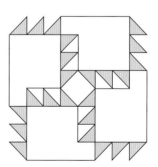

3. Fold over all the little triangles within and around the motif.

WILD GOOSE CHASE

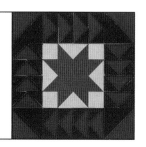

Here are just a few of the pattern variations from a very large flock of Wild Goose Chase designs. In each block, the geese are constructed of triangles (triangles represent birds in many quilt patterns). For Card Design 1 the eight geese are individual squares of paper, each one folded to resemble a tiny envelope. On Card Design 2 a cut and folded square of Wild Goose motifs chase around a central star. All the duplex papers used for these designs were white on the reverse side of a color.

MATERIALS

For each 4" (10.2-cm) card, Design 1 or 2

Equipment in the Work Box, pages 13–15

Envelope, 4¼ by 5⅛" (10.8 by 13.0-cm), or Envelope A pattern, page 104, and instructions, pages 103–104

card design 1

Photocopy of the Design 1 patterns, page 121

4 by 8" (10.2 by 20.4-cm) piece of text-weight paper, scored and folded to make a 4" (10.2-cm) square card

Four different 2 by 3" (5.1 by 7.6-cm) pieces of origami paper (white on one side of each)

card design 2

Photocopy of the Design 2 patterns, page 121

4 by 8" (10.2 by 20.4-cm) piece of text-weight duplex paper, scored and folded, with the color inside, to make a 4" (10.2-cm) square card

2" (5.1-cm) square of paper for the star

3" (7.6-cm) square of paper for inside the card

INSTRUCTIONS
card design 1

1. Rough-cut both rectangular patterns. Stack and tape together two of the origami paper pieces and tape one pattern on top. Use a pin to pierce the dot at the center of each square, then cut them out. Repeat the process with the remaining pattern and origami papers. Fold each square into a Wild Goose (Drawing 1).

2. Lightly draw a 2" (5.1-cm) square at the center of the card front. Refer to the photo and glue the geese in place.

card design 2

1. Cut the pattern precisely on the 4" (10.2-cm) square outline. Tape the unfolded card paper on the work surface vertically with the color side up.

2. Center and glue the 3" (7.6-cm) square of paper inside the card on the bottom panel (Drawing 2). On the inside top panel, align the edges of the pattern with the edges of the card.

3. Use a small pin to pierce the pattern and the paper exactly at the end of every cutting line circled in Drawing 2. Pierce the corners of the motif square, too.

4. Cut precisely to the ends of all the solid cutting lines. Remove and reserve the pattern and refer to it to score all the folding lines. Close the card, and referring to the photo for Card Design 2, fold back all the wings (red in the photo).

5. Rough-cut the center star pattern and tape it to the remaining small paper square. Cut out the star and glue it in place at the center of the card.

(L to R): Wild Goose Chase Card Design 2, Garland, Card Design 1

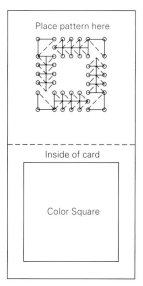

Place pattern here

Inside of card

Color Square

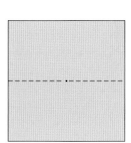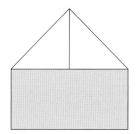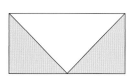

1. For Card Design 1, fold the square in half horizontally and vertically with the color inside and unfold it so the color faces up. Fold down each corner to meet the center pinhole. Fold down the top point to meet the lower edge.

2. For Card Design 2, pierce the end of every cutting line on the pattern.

WILD GOOSE CHASE

MATERIALS

garland

For one 44" (111.5-cm) garland

Two photocopies of the garland pattern, page 121

Equipment in the Work Box, pages 13–15

Four different 4½" (11.4-cm) squares of text-weight paper

Monofilament

INSTRUCTIONS

garland

1. Rough-cut both patterns for the garland pieces. Stack and tape together two of the paper squares and tape one pattern on top. Use a pin to pierce the dot at the center of each square, then cut out the pieces right through the pattern and the paper. Repeat the process with the remaining pattern and papers.

2. Prefold each square once diagonally to make triangles. Line up the triangles in a pleasing color sequence on the work surface.

3. Thread a needle with a very long piece of monofilament, then tie it in the needle's eye.

4. To place the first triangle, unfold it and thread the needle into the center pinhole from the reverse side of the paper (inside surface of the folded triangle). Slide the square down the length of monofilament bringing it to about 6" (15.2-cm) from the end. Place the square (unfolded triangle), reverse side up on the work surface and spread glue on it. Refold the triangle, sandwiching the monofilament between the two layers of folded paper. Adjust the placement so the monofilament aligns with the tip of the triangle. String the rest of the unfolded triangles on the monofilament, pulling down one at a time. The point of each new triangle should touch the pinhole of each previously placed triangle.

Card Tricks: Amish Design

Two examples of traditional Amish quilt works are re-created here in paper to honor the extraordinary artists who made the wool and cotton originals more than one hundred years ago. The strong graphic qualities of Amish quilts bring to mind the geometric paintings of Josef Albers, who explored the inter-action of color and light nearly 50 years later in his series, "Homage to the Square." This connection between intellectual twentieth-century abstract art and ingenuous nineteenth-century American quilts was celebrated in Jonathan Holstein's 1970 exhibit, "Abstract Design in American Quilts" at the Whitney Museum of Art in New York. The event was a turning point, creating an international appreciation for American quilts and causing the humble bed covering to be viewed as artwork and social document.

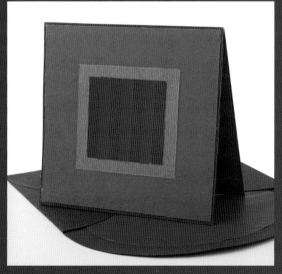

MATERIALS

For one 4" (10.2-cm) square card, Diamond or Bar

Equipment in the Work Box, pages 13–15

Envelope, 4¼ by 5⅛" (10.8 by 13.0-cm), or Envelope A pattern, page 104, and instructions, pages 103–104

amish diamond card

4 by 8" (10.2 by 20.4-cm) piece of red paper, scored and folded to make a 4" (10.2-cm) square card

3⅞" (9.8-cm) square of blue paper

2¾" (7.0-cm) square of red paper

2¼" (5.7-cm) square of blue-green paper

1⁹⁄₁₆" (4.0-cm) square of blue paper

1¹⁄₁₆" (2.7-cm) square of red paper

amish bar card

4 by 8" (10.2 by 20.4-cm) piece of magenta paper, scored and folded to make a 4" (10.2-cm) square card

3⅞" (9.8-cm) square of avocado green paper

2¼" (5.7-cm) square of dark turquoise paper

1¾" (4.4-cm) square of magenta paper

Three ¼" by 1¾" (0.6-cm) strips of blue-violet paper

INSTRUCTIONS

There are no patterns for these designs, because the patches are cut to size. Referring to the photos, stack, center, and glue them on the cards.

RAIL FENCE

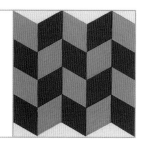

The intentional repeat pattern of two zingy colors gives this diamond design the look of a contemporary folding screen. The very same pattern, pieced with randomly placed colors and prints, has been found in quilts dating all the way back to the eighteeth century. Through the years (more than two hundred of them!) several variations on this motif have evolved. Based on the color placement and the angle of the diamond patch, the pattern has been called Rail Fence, Zig Zag, Wave, Streak of Lightning, Herringbone, and Hit and Miss Variation.

MATERIALS

For one 4¼" (10.8-cm) square card

Photocopy of the patterns, page 125

Equipment in the Work Box, pages 13–15

4¼ by 8½" (10.8 by 21.6-cm) piece of cardstock, scored and folded to make a 4¼" (10.8-cm) square card

2½ by 3¼" (6.4 by 8.3-cm) piece of paper (the same color on each side) for the Stripes Unit

Two 2½ by 3" (6.4 by 7.6-cm) pieces of paper for the A and B Piece Units

Envelope, 4⅜ by 5¾" (11.1 by 14.6-cm), or Envelope B pattern, page 105, and instructions, pages 103–104

Rail Fence Card

INSTRUCTIONS

1. Cut out the photocopied card pattern precisely on the outline. Use a pin to pierce each crevice and point along the top and bottom edges of the motif drawn on the pattern.

2. Align the edges of the pattern with the card and use paper clips to hold the two pieces together. Place the point of a very sharp pencil in each pinhole, then remove the pattern. Connect the dots with light pencil lines to re-create the outline of the motif on the card front. Put the card aside.

3. Rough-cut the Stripes Unit pattern and tape it to the 2½ by 3¼" (6.4 by 8.3-cm) piece of paper. Cut the pattern on all the solid lines to make four individual stripes and put them aside.

4. Precisely cut out the A Piece Unit pattern and attach it to one of the two identical remaining pieces of paper with tape placed along the pattern's short edges.

Note the three rows of dotted placement lines on the pattern and use a straight-edge and solid pencil lines to extend these lines beyond the pattern and onto the colored paper. Remove one of the two pieces of tape and, using the remaining piece of tape as a hinge, lift up the pattern so the placement lines can be connected and drawn under it. Note the placement of the stripes on the pattern and glue two of the reserved stripes in place. The stripes are cut extra-long. After the glue is completely dry, fold down the hinged pattern and tape it in place over the stripes. Cut on all the solid lines of the pattern to make three striped A pieces.

5. Repeat Step 4 using the B Piece Unit pattern, noting that the stripes are placed in a different position on the B Unit.

6. Referring to the photo and the pattern and using the pencil guidelines, glue three A and two B pieces in place on the card front.

6

WHIRLING HEXAGONS AND OCTAGON DESIGN

The six-sided hexagon is one of the most versatile of geometric shapes for patchwork. Cutting it in half produces two trapezoid shapes and slicing it like a pie makes six equilateral triangles. Hexagons mix well with diamonds and triangles to create intricate star and snowflake motifs. Many quilt designs start with a single hexagon patch and develop into flower, wave, and honeycomb patterns as additional hexagons are fitted like puzzle pieces around the original one at the center. The eight-sided octagon is not as versatile as a hexagon, but it plays well with squares and right-angle triangles to create stars, wreaths, and cobweb designs.

Whirling Hexagons (page 92)

HEXAGON PATCHWORK

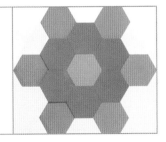

Hexagon Patchwork has at least thirty other names, perhaps because the six-sided patch presents so many design possibilities. One can combine colors and arrange prints randomly (Hit and Miss and Honeycomb) or purposefully (Colonial Bouquet and Mosaic). Vermont's Shelburne Museum has an 1813 Hit and Miss quilt and a Mosaic quilt from 1850. During the quilting revival of the 1930s, Mosaic made quite a comeback, complete with a new name, Grandmother's Flower Garden. In Carrie Hall's 1930s book, *The Romance of the Patchwork Quilt,* this "very popular and modern" design is pictured in a vintage photograph of a "Garden" quilt containing more than eight thousand pieces! The author also included a photograph of a somewhat similar 1875 Mosaic quilt, suggesting that it was the "grandmother" of Grandmother's Flower Garden.

MATERIALS

card

For one 4 ⅝ by 4-inch (11.8 by 10.1-cm) card

Photocopies of the three card patterns, page 122

Equipment in the Work Box, pages 13–15

5 by 9-inch (12.7 by 22.9-cm) piece of paper, scored, and folded to make a 5 by 4½-inch (12.7 by 11.4-cm) card

3½-inch (8.9-cm) square of paper for the flower

1¾-inch (4.4-cm) square of paper for the flower center

Envelope, 4¼ by 5⅛ (10.8 by 13.0-cm), or Envelope A pattern, page 104, and instructions, pages 103–104

Top: Hexagon Patchwork Boxes; Bottom (L to R): Hexagon Patchwork Card, Hexagon Patchwork Box With Flower Motif Top

INSTRUCTIONS

card

1. Rough-cut the card leaf pattern. Trim the pattern on the outline only along the two top "place-on-fold" edges. Tape the pattern in place on the folded card aligning the top of the pattern with the folded edge. Cut out the card right through the pattern and put the card aside.

2. Rough-cut the flower pattern and tape it to the flower paper. Use a pin to pierce a single hole at the end of each cutting line circled on the pattern.

3. Cutting directly through the pattern, make six slices into the flower to create petals. Cut out the flower shape and flip it to the reverse side of the paper. Score the distance between the pinholes to create a scored hexagon shape at the center. Extend the petal cutting lines to meet the pinholes, if necessary. Flip the paper again to the right side, fold up the petals some-what, and put the flower aside.

4. Rough-cut the flower center pattern and tape it to the flower center paper. Cut directly through the pattern to make the center hexagon shape and glue it on the reserved flower. Glue the flower on the reserved card, referring to the photo for placement.

HEXAGON PATCHWORK

MATERIALS

box

For one 2⅛ by 2½ by 1¼-inch
(5.4 by 6.4 by 3.2-cm) box

Photocopy of the Box pattern, page 123

Equipment in the Work Box, pages 13–15

7½ by 8½-inch (19.1 by 21.6-cm) piece of
cardstock or scrapbooking paper

box top flower motif

Photocopy of the box top motif pattern,
page 123

2½-inch (6.4-cm) square of paper for the
leaf portion

2-inch (5.1-cm) square of paper for the
flower

1½-inch (3.8-cm) square of paper for the
flower center

INSTRUCTIONS

box

1. Rough-cut the box pattern. Tape the
pattern to the side of the paper that will
be outside the box. Cut right through the
pattern to cut out the box shape.

2. Referring to the pattern, score and crease
the box on all the folding lines. Spread
glue on the outside surface of the glue tab
adjacent to Panel 1 and press the tab
under Panel 6. Glue the base tabs inside
the box to add strength to the container.
Put the box aside.

3. To make the optional box top flower motif,
rough-cut the photocopied pattern and
tape it to the leaf paper, cut out the
shaded leaf shape (Drawing 1) directly
through the pattern, reserve the pattern,
and put the leaf aside.

4. Tape the reserved pattern to the flower
paper. Use a pin to pierce a hole at the
end of each cutting line circled on Drawing
2 and cut out the shaded flower shape,
slicing into the flower to make the petals.
Reserve the pattern. Flip the cut out
flower to the reverse side of the paper.
Score the distance between the pinholes
to create a scored hexagon shape at the
center of the flower. Extend the petal
cutting lines to meet the pinholes if
necessary. Turn the flower to the right
side of the paper, lift the petals, and put
the flower aside.

5. Tape the reserved pattern to the flower
center paper, cut out the shaded hexagon
(Drawing 3), and glue it on the flower.
Glue the flower on the leaf, then center
and glue the motif on the box top so the
outside edges of both the motif and the
box are parallel.

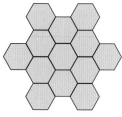

1. Cut out the leaf shape.

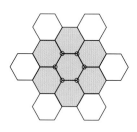

2. Cut out the shaded flower.

3. Cut out the center.

Card Tricks: Cobweb

This is a quick-to-make card, a spin-off inspired by traditional Cobweb and Spider Web designs. Triangles and kite-shaped patches are cut from striped paper and arranged to form an octagon pattern that also resembles a beach umbrella. For accuracy, precise placement and cutting of the stripes is a must, so cut all the card patches at one time.

MATERIALS

For one 4¼-inch (10.8-cm) card

Photocopy of the pattern, page 126

Equipment in the Work Box, pages 13–15

4½ by 9-inch (11.4 by 22.9-cm) piece of cardstock, scored and folded to make a 4 ½-inch (11.4-cm) card

3¾ by 7½-inch (9.5 by 19.0-cm) piece of striped paper, stripes running the length of the paper

4¼ by 8-inch (10.8 by 20.3-cm) piece of the same striped paper, stripes running the length of the paper

4½-inch (11.4-cm) square of graph paper

Envelope, 4⅜ by 5¾-inch (11.1 by 14.6-cm), or Envelope B pattern, page 105, and instructions, pages 103–104

INSTRUCTIONS

1. Stack and tape the small piece of paper on top of the larger one, aligning the stripes perfectly.

2. Cut out the pattern rectangle on its outline and place it on the striped stack of paper. Align the base cutting line of the triangles and the dotted line on the kite-shaped pieces along the bottom edge of one of the dominant stripes. Tape the pattern in place.

3. Cut out the octagon segments, slicing directly through the pattern and the two layers of paper. There will be four triangles and four kite-shaped pieces. To avoid confusion, put the scraps aside for another use.

4. Draw a 4¼-inch (10.8-cm) square on the graph paper. Fit the four kite-shaped pieces into the corners of the square and the four triangles between them, around the sides. Hold the pieces in place with paper clips. The sharp points of the segments should meet at the center. Adjust if necessary. Glue the eight pieces in place on the graph paper.

5. Trim one edge of the graph paper square along one edge of the motif. Align the trimmed edge with the folding line of the card and glue the card and motif together. When dry, trim the remaining edges of the graph paper to match the edges of the motif.

WHIRLING HEXAGONS

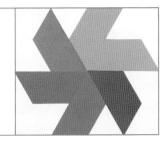

Whirling Hexagons was one of the more than one thousand full-size quilt patterns published weekly in the *Kansas City Star* from 1928–1960. Its beauty is in its charming simplicity and playful versatility. The result of interlocking the Whirling Hexagons or clustering them together brings to mind two of nature's wondrous creations, the spider web and the snowflake.

MATERIALS

Common Materials for one 4¼ by 5" (10.8 by 12.7-cm) card

Equipment in the Work Box, pages 13–15

Envelope, 4⅜ by 5¾" (11.1 by 14.6-cm), or Envelope B pattern, page 105, and instructions, pages 103–104

design 1

Photocopy of Design 1 pattern, page 124

5½ by 9" (14.0 by 22.9-cm) piece of cardstock, scored and folded to make a 4½ by 5½" (11.4 by 14.0-cm) card

Five different 1½ by 3" (3.8 by 7.6-cm) pieces of compatibly colored paper (card will provide sixth color)

design 2

Photocopy of Design 2 pattern, page 124

5½ by 9" (14.0 by 22.9-cm) piece of cardstock, scored and folded to make a 4½ by 5½" (11.4 by 22.9-cm) card

Six different 2½" (6.4-cm) squares of compatibly colored paper (card will provide seventh color at the center)

design 3

Photocopy of Design 3 pattern, page 125

4¾ by 9" (12.1 by 22.9-cm) piece of cardstock, scored and folded to make a 4½ by 4¾" (11.4 by 12.1-cm) card

4½ by 4¾" (11.4 by 12.1-cm) piece of contrasting paper for inside the card

Top: Whirling Hexagons Card Design 1; Bottom (L to R): Card Design 3, Card Design 2

INSTRUCTIONS

design 1

1. Rough-cut the pattern. Precisely trim only the top edge along the "place-on-fold" line. Tape the folded card onto the work surface. Tape the pattern onto the card, aligning the trimmed edge of the pattern with the folded edge at the top of the card.

2. Cut around the outline, right through the pattern and the card. Reserve the pattern and use it to cut each differently-colored wing of the Whirling Hexagon. Glue the pieces on the card in a pleasing color sequence.

design 2

1. Rough-cut the pattern. Precisely trim only the top edge along the "place-on-fold" line. Highlight the outside edge of the pattern motif to minimize the chance of a cutting error. Tape the folded card onto the work surface. Tape the pattern on top of the card, aligning the trimmed edge of the pattern with the folded edge of the card.

2. Use a pin to pierce the pattern and cardstock at every point and crevice that is circled on the pattern. These tiny pinholes will help you place and glue the small hexagons around the edge of the card.

3. Reserve the card pattern and use it to cut each differently colored small hexagon. Glue the pieces on the card in a pleasing color sequence.

design 3

1. Rough-cut the pattern. All the little triangles on the pattern are shaded to minimize the chance of cutting errors. Precisely trim only the top edge along the "place-on-fold" line.

2. Unfold the cardstock and tape it right side up on the work surface. Tape the pattern onto the card front, aligning the trimmed edge of the pattern with the folding line of the card.

3. Cutting out the shaded triangle areas of this design requires complete concentration. Although a transparent plastic straightedge is not as safe as a metal one, being able to see through the straightedge is an advantage here. While cutting the design, the center hexagon will be cut free. Remove and reserve it, marking the top so it can later be placed correctly inside the card.

4. Cut out the card front around the pattern outline, but not along the folding line. Remove the pattern from the card and the card from the work surface.

5. Refold the card and hold the front and back layers together with removable tape or paper clips. Trim away the card back paper so it aligns with the front.

6. Unfold the card and glue the contrasting paper on the inside back surface, trimming it to align with the edges of the card. Refold the card and center and glue the reserved hexagon in place.

SEVEN SISTERS

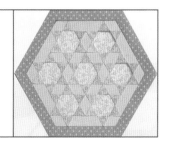

Because of its clear visibility in the night sky, the cluster of stars known as the Seven Sisters is part of the folklore of ancient and modern cultures alike. It surely must have been the inspiration for this quilt pattern, seen as early as 1845. The arrangement of six stars surrounding the center star creates a secondary diamond design, somewhat like a snowflake.

MATERIALS

For one 5 by 4¼" (12.7 by 10.8-cm) card

Photocopy of the pattern, page 126

Equipment in the Work Box, pages 13–15

5½ by 9" (14.0 by 22.9-cm) piece of duplex paper, scored and folded to make a 5½ by 4½" (14.0 by 11.4-cm) card

5½ by 4½" (14.0 by 11.4-cm) piece of paper for the border, optional.

Envelope, 4⅜ by 5¾" (11.1 by 14.6-cm), or Envelope B pattern, page 105, and instructions, pages 103–104

Seven Sisters Cards

INSTRUCTIONS

1. Rough-cut the photocopied pattern. Highlight the six sets of "pie-slice" solid cutting lines to minimize the possibility of cutting errors. Precisely trim only the top edge of the pattern along the "place-on-fold" line.

2. Unfold the card paper and tape it on the work surface so the folding line is horizontal and the star color is facing up (actually the inside surface of the card). Tape the pattern on the card paper so the trimmed top edge of the pattern aligns with the folding line of the card.

3. Use a pin to pierce through the pattern and card at the end of every line circled on the pattern. The pinholes will provide guide points when scoring the card in the next step. Cut each of the seven little "pies" into slices on the solid cutting lines.

4. Cut out the card front around the pattern edge, but not along the folding line. Remove the pattern from the card, but leave the card taped to the work surface. Reserve the pattern if making a border. If the ends of the cut "slices" do not reach the corresponding pinholes, extend them. Referring to the pattern, score the broken lines (folding lines) between the six pinholes around each star, forming a hexagon.

5. Remove the card from the work surface and refold it, holding the front and back layers together with removable tape or paper clips. Trim away the card back paper so the edges align with the shape of the card front. Fold back the points of each star. For the optional border, tape the reserved pattern to the paper of choice, cut out the border, and glue it in place on the card front.

LATTICE BLOCK

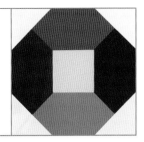

With its open space at the center, the Lattice Block was just the kind of pattern chosen for a Friendship or Signature quilt. Each block of a Friendship quilt was usually made by a different person who signed the center of the block with indelible ink or embroidery stitches to create a gift quilt. Friends and family worked together to create this kind of gift quilt for a bride or a beloved neighbor moving away from the community. To quickly cut accurate squares for each of the designs, stack and tape together three or four layers of origami paper. Tape a piece of graph paper to the top and use it to precisely measure, mark, and cut the square patches.

MATERIALS

Common Materials for one 4" (10.2-cm) square or octagon card

Equipment in the Work Box, pages 13–15

4 by 8" (10.2 by 20.4-cm) piece of card stock, scored and folded to make a 4" (10.2-cm) square card

Envelope, 4¼ by 5⅛" (10.8 by 13.0-cm), or Envelope A pattern, page 104, and instructions, pages 103–104

design 1

Four 2" (5.1-cm) squares of origami or text-weight paper, each a different color

design 2

Sixteen 1" (2.5-cm) squares of origami or text-weight paper, two each of eight different colors

Top: Lattice Block Card Design 1; Bottom (L to R): Card Design 2, Card Design 1

INSTRUCTIONS

design 1

1. Use a pencil to lightly draw horizontal and vertical lines directly on the card front to divide the square into quarter sections. Set the card aside.

2. Fold each of the 2-inch (5.1-cm) paper squares, making four units for the motif (Drawings 1–3). Referring to the photograph, glue the four units on the card front to create the motif.

3. Following the edges of the motif, cut the corners off the folded card to make an octagon shape.

4. Unfold the card and cut out the square center, again following the edges of the motif.

design 2

1. Lightly draw a grid of sixteen squares on the card front. Put the card aside.

2. Fold each 1" (2.5-cm) paper square, making sixteen units (Drawings 1–3). Arrange the units on the card front and glue them in place.

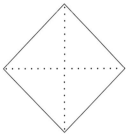

1. Mark the center point on the reverse side of each origami square by drawing criss-crossed diagonal lines from corner to corner.

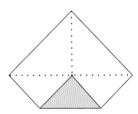

2. Fold a corner of the square to the center point.

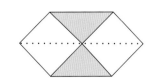

3. Fold the opposite corner to the center point.

CASTLE WALL

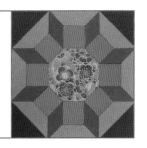

Create a dimensional effect for the Castle Wall motif by experimenting with color, texture, and contrasting dark and light papers. A second motif is concealed within the Castle Wall, known as Venetian Block or Ferris Wheel. This additional pattern is offered as a dimensional ornament instead of a note card, and it really does look like a little Ferris wheel when completed.

MATERIALS

card

For one 4 ¼" (10.8-cm) square card

Photocopy of the pattern, page 127

Equipment in the Work Box, pages 13–15

4½ by 9" (11.4 by 22.8-cm) piece of cardstock, scored and folded to make a 4½" (11.4-cm) square card

4½" (11.4-cm) square of paper for Layer 1, the large octagon

4½" (11.4-cm) square of paper for Layer 2, the star

4½" (11.4-cm) square of paper for Layer 3, the notched octagon

3¾" (9.5-cm) square of paper for Layer 4, the center octagon

Envelope, 4⅜ by 5¾" (11.1 by 14.6-cm), or Envelope B pattern, page 105, and instructions, pages 103–104

INSTRUCTIONS

card

1. Cut out the photocopied pattern precisely on the square outline. Clip it to the folded card, aligning the side edge of the pattern with the fold at the side of the card. Draw around the square shape of the pattern, but do not cut the cardstock at this time. Remove and reserve the pattern. It will be used for each subsequent layer of the design.

2. To allow for cutting variations when fitting all the layers together, place the paper being cut and the card being made side-by-side on the work surface. As each piece is cut from the paper, lift it up, move it to the card, and glue it in exactly the same position, building the design layer by layer as you work.

3. Tape the pattern to the paper selected for Layer 1. Highlight the outline of the large white octagon shape to provide a cutting pathway (Drawing 1). Cut on the large octagon outline directly through the pattern and the paper, trimming away the shaded area (Drawing 1). Remove and reserve the pattern. Glue Layer 1 on the card.

4. Tape the reserved pattern to the paper selected for Layer 2. Highlight the outline of the star-shaped area (Drawing 2). Cut on the large star-shaped outline, trimming away the shaded area (Drawing 2). Remove and reserve the pattern. Glue Layer 2 on Layer 1.

5. Tape the reserved pattern to the paper selected for Layer 3. Highlight the notched octagon, cutting around the shape and trimming away the shaded portion (Drawing 3). Remove and reserve the pattern. Glue Layer 3 on Layer 2.

6. Tape the same pattern to the paper selected for Layer 4. Highlight and cut out the center octagon, trimming away the shaded area (Drawing 4). Glue Layer 4 on Layer 3. Trim the card on the penciled square outline.

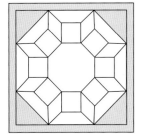

1. Cut away the shaded area to make the octagon for Layer 1.

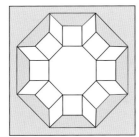

2. Cut away the shaded area to make the star shape for Layer 2.

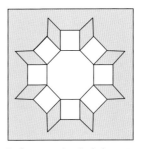

3. Cut away the shaded area to make the notched octagon for Layer 3.

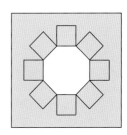

4. Cut away the shaded area to make the center octagon for Layer 4.

CASTLE WALL

MATERIALS

ferris wheel ornament

For one 3¼" (8.3-cm) diameter ornament

Photocopy of the pattern, page 127

Equipment in the Work Box, pages 13–15

4½ by 7" (11.4 by 17.8-cm) piece of medium-weight paper

10" (25.4-cm) length of monofilament

INSTRUCTIONS

ferris wheel ornament

1. Rough-cut the pattern and tape it on the right side of the ornament paper. In order to transfer the folding lines, use a pin to pierce the dots circled on the pattern. Tape the paper onto the work surface.

2. Cut the piece on all the solid lines of the pattern, slicing through both the pattern and the paper. Remove the pattern, but leave the paper taped in place on the work surface. Score the four long parallel mountain fold lines (M) on the right side surface of the paper. Flip the piece over to the reverse side. If the cutting lines do not meet the pinholes, extend them. Using the cutting lines as guidelines, score all of the short valley fold lines (V) on both core areas.

3. Flip the piece back to the right side. Crease all of the long mountain folds. Crease all of the short valley folds.

4. On the right side of the paper, spread glue along one of the shaded core areas, avoiding the tab. Fold the piece lengthwise along the scored parallel lines to make a boxy segmented tube. Overlap the glue-covered area with the other shaded area to create the core of the ornament. The small tabs should not be glued together.

5. Spread apart the two tabs at the one end of the core area. Place glue on the inside surface of both tabs, but do not stick them together. Holding the tabs apart in one hand, and the opposite end of the core in the other hand, form an octagonal doughnut, bringing the ends of the core together and overlapping them as you place one glue tab inside the core and the other tab outside the core. Thread the piece of monofilament through the ornament and tie the ends in a knot.

PATTERNS

Here are all the patterns for all the card designs with their envelopes, and the spin-off projects they inspired. Photocopying these patterns will save you some tracing time, simplify the cutting process, and ensure accuracy. Soon you will be stuffing quilt-filled envelopes into your mailbox in record time!

MAKING ENVELOPES

Creating custom envelopes is a quick and easy task once you've made the patterns. It's also fun because of the unlimited choices of color, texture, and size. In order to be acceptable for mailing, envelopes must conform to certain postal standards regarding minimum size, proper height-to-length ratio, and maximum thickness of contents. To avoid postal surcharges or delivery delays due to returned unacceptable envelopes, visit your post office and request information about current standards or ask for a photocopy of the template that clerks use to check mail dimensions.

MATERIALS

For one envelope A, B, or C

Pattern of choice, pages 104–105

Equipment in the Work Box, pages 13–15

Graph paper or tracing paper

Paper of choice (size requirements listed on each pattern)

Acetate, optional

INSTRUCTIONS

1. Trace the rectangular envelope pattern in the size of your choice. Also make two tracings of the semicircle for the top and bottom flap and two tracings of the semi-circular side flap. For the greatest accuracy, draw on graph paper and use a compass to trace the semicircles. Cut out all the pattern pieces (Drawing 1).

2. Arrange the pattern pieces in the proper order on your work surface and tape them together. Practice folding the envelope pattern to check the alignment of the flaps (Drawing 2). To add strength to the pattern, glue it to acetate and cut it out.

3. Trace the pattern for the optional liner circle on folded paper and cut it out (Drawing 3, next page).

4. Place a square or rectangle of the selected paper right-side up on the work surface. Tape or clip the pattern onto the paper and draw around the pattern shape. Remove the pattern. Draw and score the perpen-dicular lines within the outlined shape to define the straight edges of the envelope. Cut out the shape (Drawing 4, next page).

5. Flip the envelope over to the reverse side of the paper. Fold the inside flaps. Apply glue to the edges of the bottom flap, avoiding the center area. Fold up the bottom flap so it overlaps the side flaps (Drawing 5, next page). To protect the interior of the envelope from misplaced glue, slide in a piece of scrap paper to keep the front and back layers separated. Remove the scrap paper just before the glue is dry.

6. Flip the optional liner over to the reverse side and apply glue only to the half of the circle above the folding line (Drawing 6, next page).

7. Slide the unglued portion of the liner inside the envelope (Drawing 7, next page). Center the glued area of the liner on the top flap, aligning the folds, and press the two layers together. Fold down the top flap to finalize the placement of the liner. In order to hinge well, the folding lines of the liner and the envelope will probably shift and not be aligned after folding and then lifting the top flap.

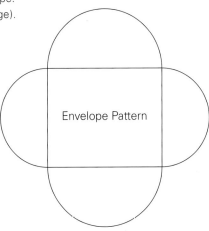

2. Tape the pattern pieces together.

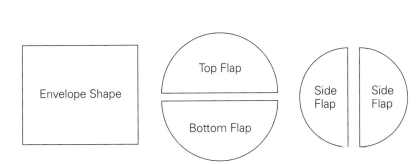

1. Trace and cut out all the pattern pieces.

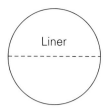

Liner

3. Fold and cut out the
optional liner pattern.

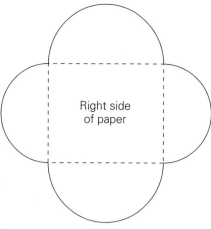

Right side
of paper

4. Draw, score and cut out the envelope.

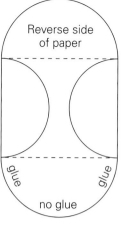

Reverse side
of paper

glue   glue

no glue

5. Apply glue and fold the flaps.

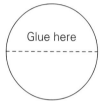

Glue here

6. On the reverse side of liner
apply glue above the folding line.

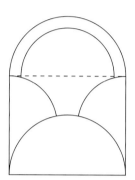

7. Slide the liner in the envelope.

ENVELOPE PATTERNS

ENVELOPE A
Final size: 4¼" by 5⅛" (10.8 by 13.0-cm)
Paper size: 9¾" (24.8-cm) square, or
8½" by 11" (21.6 by 27.9-cm)
rectangle (diagonally)

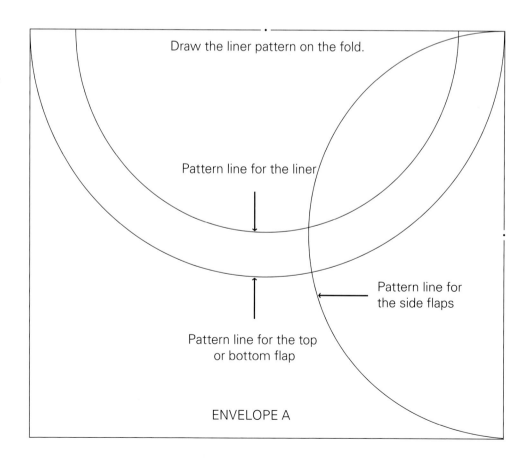

Draw the liner pattern on the fold.

Pattern line for the liner

Pattern line for
the side flaps

Pattern line for the top
or bottom flap

ENVELOPE A

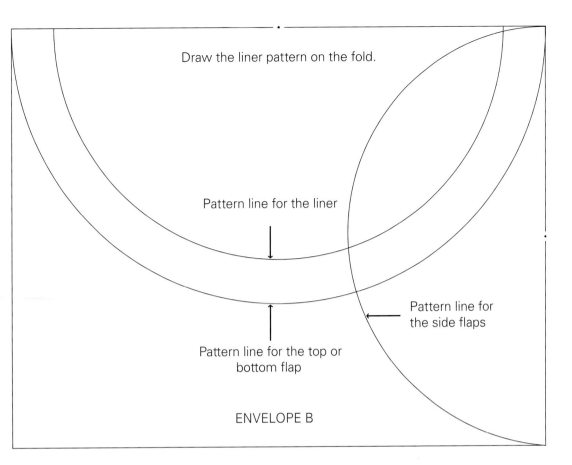

Draw the liner pattern on the fold.

Pattern line for the liner

Pattern line for
the side flaps

Pattern line for the top or
bottom flap

ENVELOPE B

ENVELOPE B
Final size: 4⅜″ by 5¾″
(11.1 by 14.6-cm
Paper size: 10½″ (26.7-cm)
square, or 9″ by 12″
(22.9 by 30.5-cm)
rectangle (diagonally

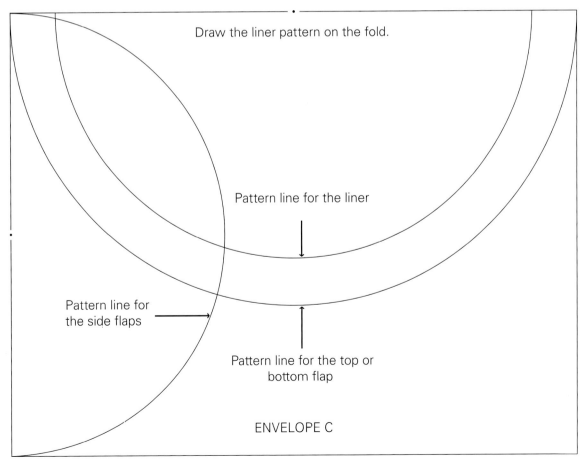

Draw the liner pattern on the fold.

Pattern line for the liner

Pattern line for
the side flaps

Pattern line for the top or
bottom flap

ENVELOPE C

ENVELOPE C
Final size: 4⅝″ by 6⅛″
(11.8 by 15.6-cm
Paper size: 11″
(27.9cm) square

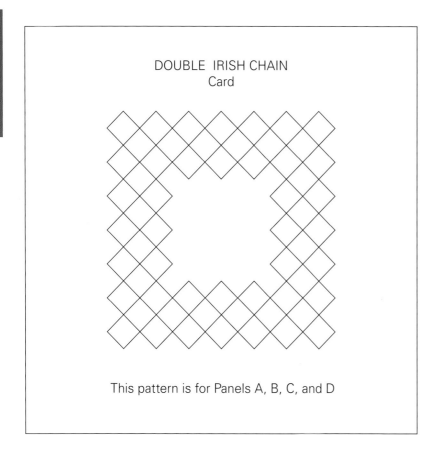

DOUBLE IRISH CHAIN
Card

This pattern is for Panels A, B, C, and D

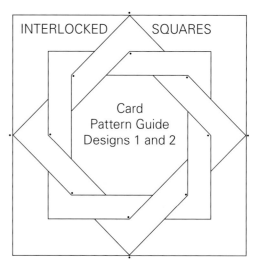

INTERLOCKED   SQUARES

Card
Pattern Guide
Designs 1 and 2

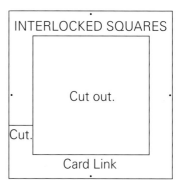

INTERLOCKED SQUARES

Cut out.

Cut.

Card Link

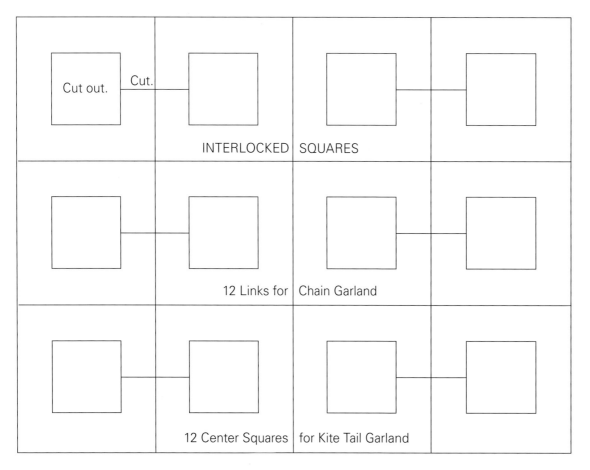

Cut out.   Cut.

INTERLOCKED SQUARES

12 Links for Chain Garland

12 Center Squares for Kite Tail Garland

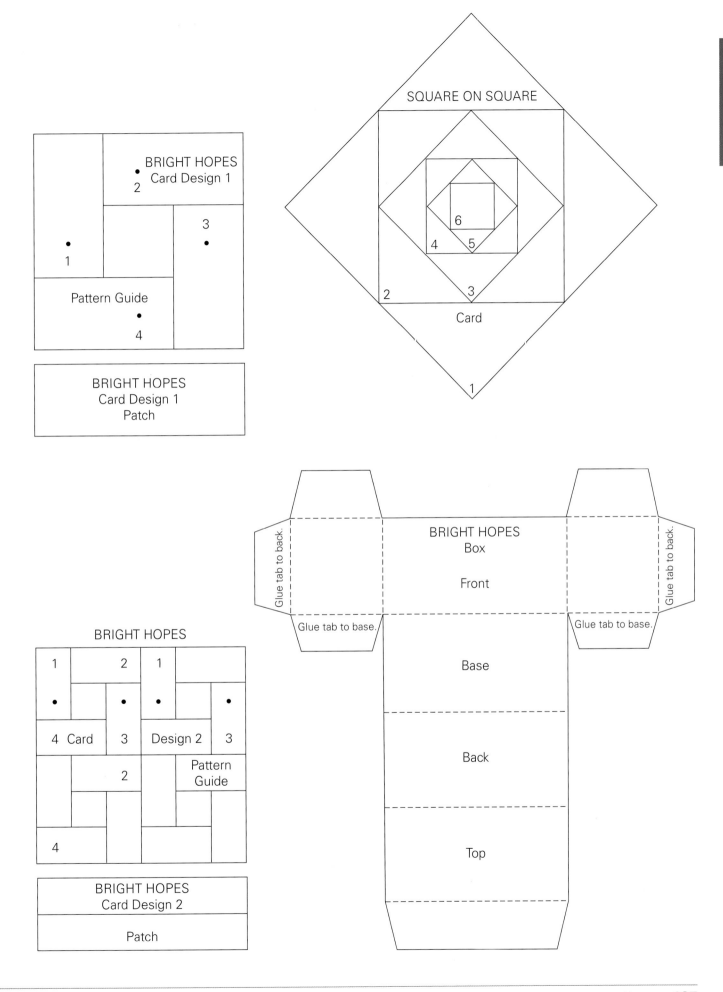

BRIGHT HOPES
Card Design 1

• 2

3 •

1 •

Pattern Guide

• 4

BRIGHT HOPES
Card Design 1
Patch

SQUARE ON SQUARE

6

4   5

2   3

Card

1

BRIGHT HOPES

1		2	1
•		•	•	•
4 Card		3	Design 2	3
	2		Pattern Guide
4			

BRIGHT HOPES
Card Design 2

Patch

BRIGHT HOPES
Box

Front

Glue tab to back.

Glue tab to back.

Glue tab to base.

Glue tab to base.

Base

Back

Top

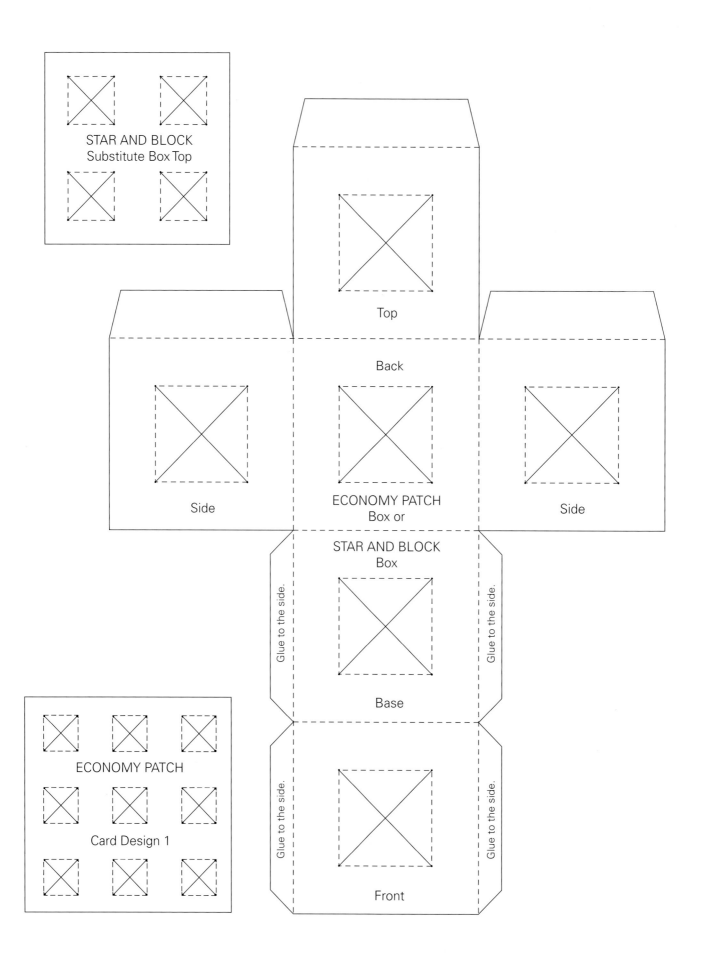

STAR AND BLOCK
Substitute Box Top

Top

Back

Side

ECONOMY PATCH
Box or

STAR AND BLOCK
Box

Side

Base

Glue to the side.

Glue to the side.

Glue to the side.

Glue to the side.

Front

ECONOMY PATCH

Card Design 1

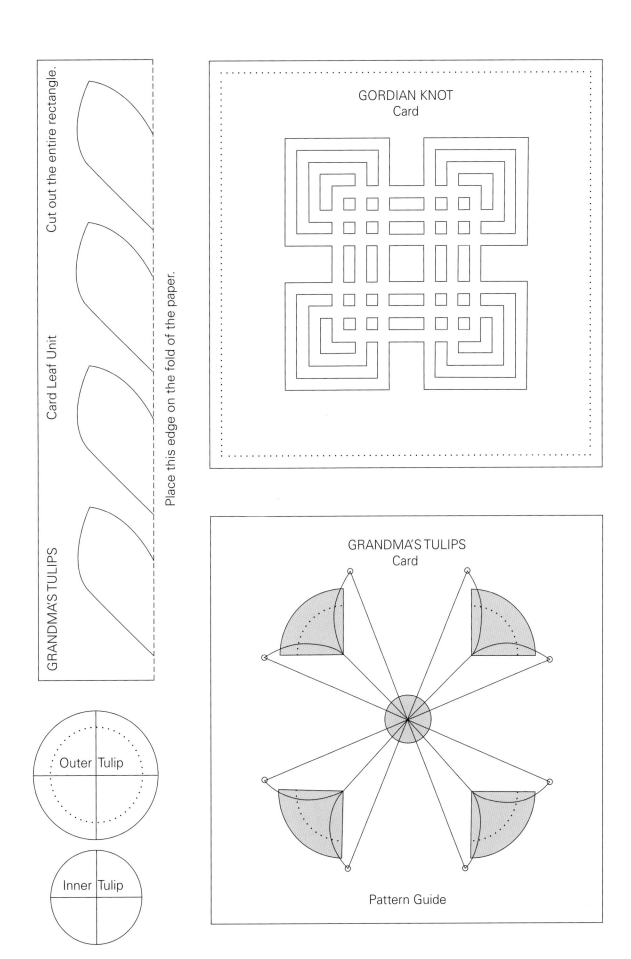

Cut out the entire rectangle.

Card Leaf Unit

GRANDMA'S TULIPS

Place this edge on the fold of the paper.

Outer Tulip

Inner Tulip

GORDIAN KNOT
Card

GRANDMA'S TULIPS
Card

Pattern Guide

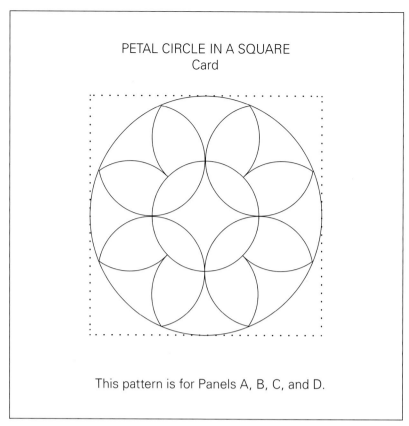

PETAL CIRCLE IN A SQUARE
Card

This pattern is for Panels A, B, C, and D.

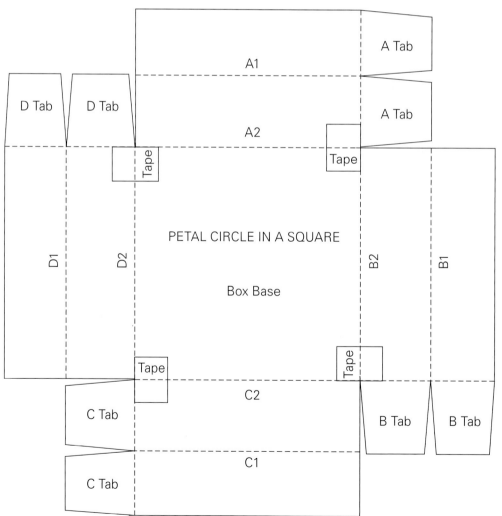

A1

A Tab

A Tab

A2

Tape

D Tab   D Tab

Tape

D1   D2

PETAL CIRCLE IN A SQUARE

B2   B1

Box Base

Tape   Tape

C2

C Tab

B Tab   B Tab

C1

C Tab

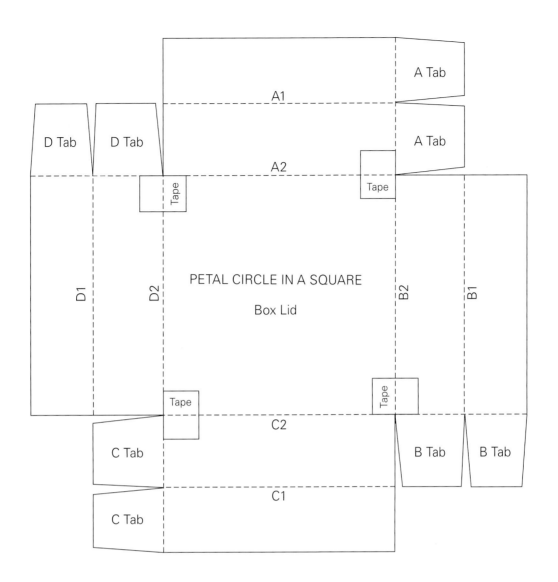

PETAL CIRCLE IN A SQUARE

Box Lid

D Tab   D Tab

A1

A Tab

A2

A Tab

Tape

Tape

D1   D2

B2   B1

Tape

Tape

C2

C Tab

B Tab   B Tab

C1

C Tab

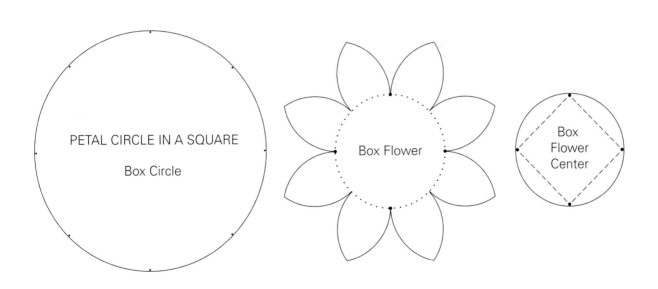

PETAL CIRCLE IN A SQUARE

Box Circle

Box Flower

Box
Flower
Center

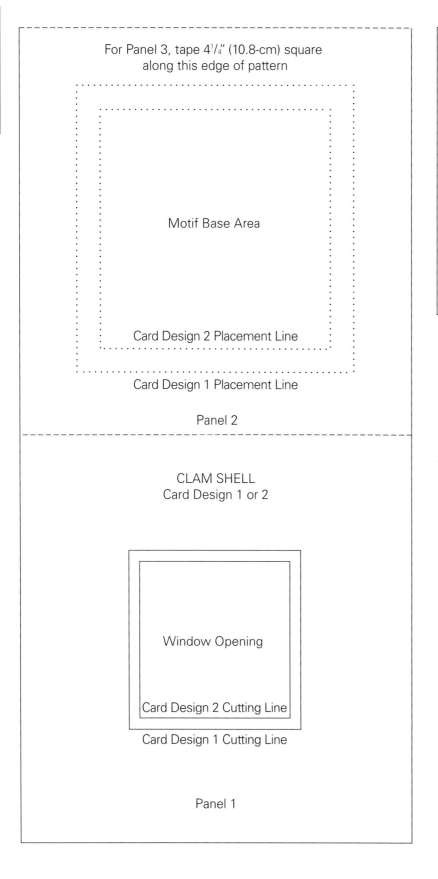

For Panel 3, tape 4¼" (10.8-cm) square
along this edge of pattern

Motif Base Area

Card Design 2 Placement Line

Card Design 1 Placement Line

Panel 2

CLAM SHELL
Card Design 1 or 2

Window Opening

Card Design 2 Cutting Line

Card Design 1 Cutting Line

Panel 1

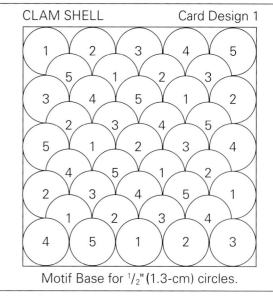

CLAM SHELL   Card Design 1

Motif Base for ½" (1.3-cm) circles.

For Panel 3, tape a 4¼" (10.8-cm) square
above Panel 2 of the Clam Shell pattern,
as shown below.

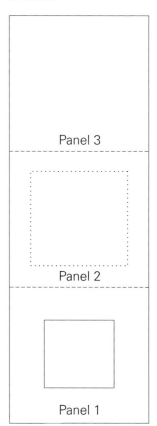

Panel 3

Panel 2

Panel 1

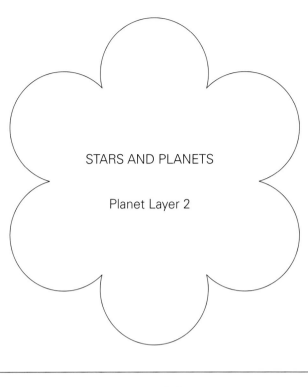

STARS AND PLANETS

Planet Layer 2

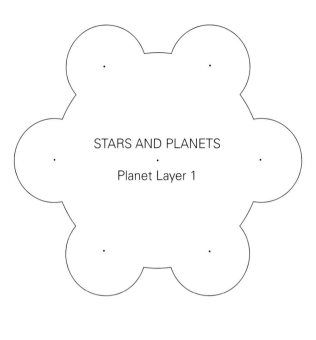

STARS AND PLANETS

Planet Layer 1

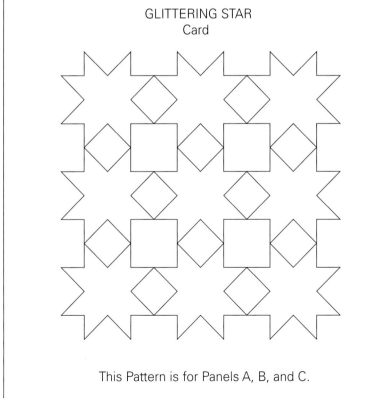

GLITTERING STAR
Card

This Pattern is for Panels A, B, and C.

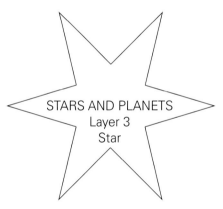

STARS AND PLANETS
Layer 3
Star

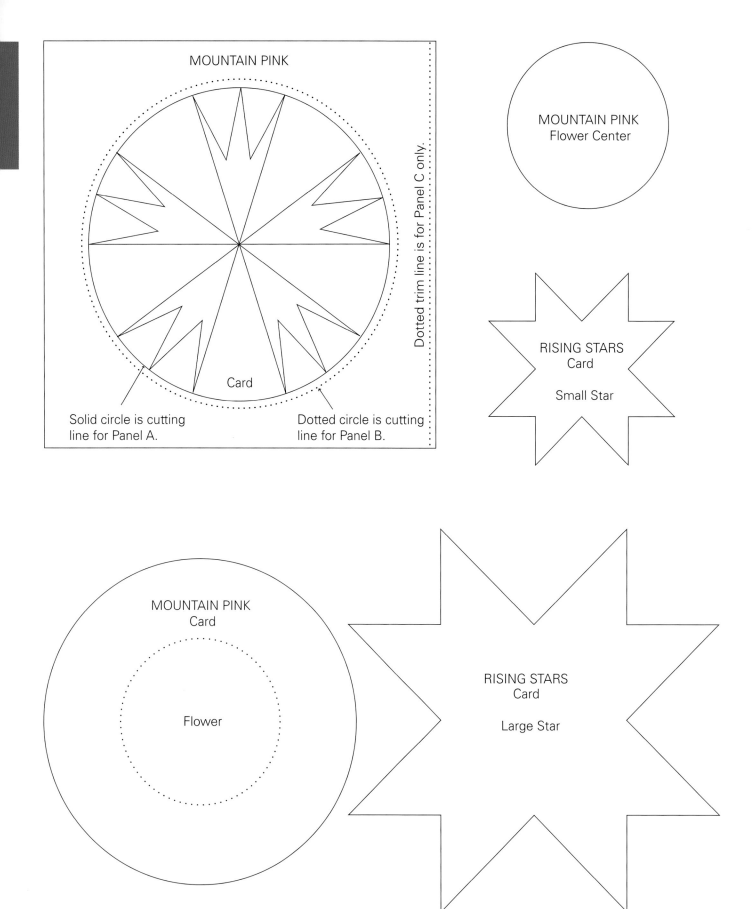

MOUNTAIN PINK

MOUNTAIN PINK
Flower Center

Card

Dotted trim line is for Panel C only.

Solid circle is cutting
line for Panel A.

Dotted circle is cutting
line for Panel B.

RISING STARS
Card

Small Star

MOUNTAIN PINK
Card

Flower

RISING STARS
Card

Large Star

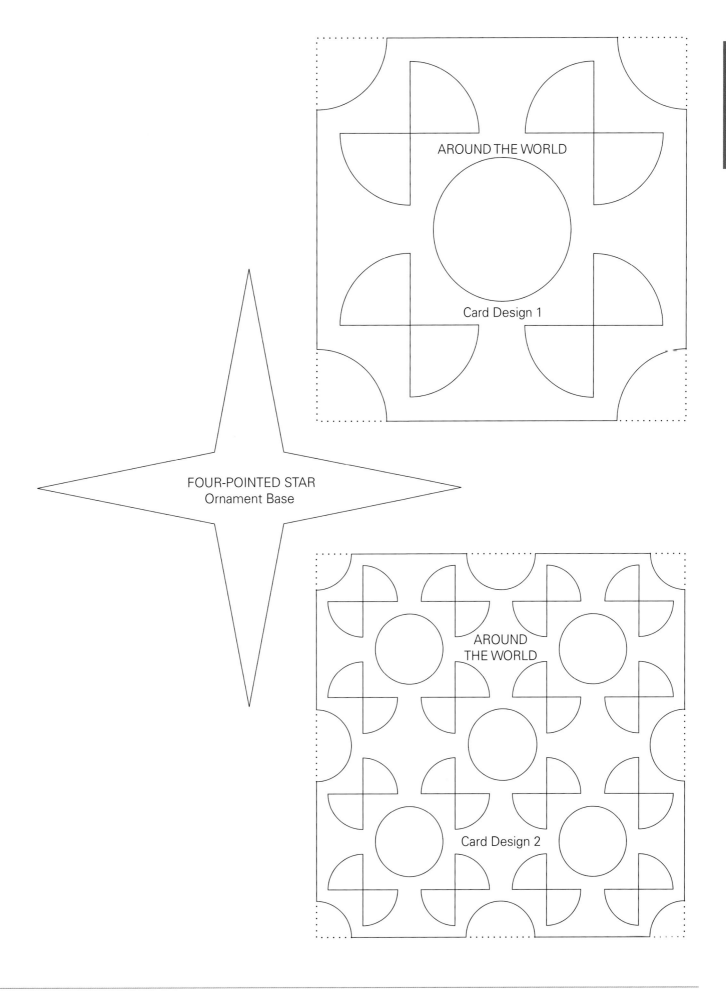

AROUND THE WORLD

Card Design 1

FOUR-POINTED STAR
Ornament Base

AROUND
THE WORLD

Card Design 2

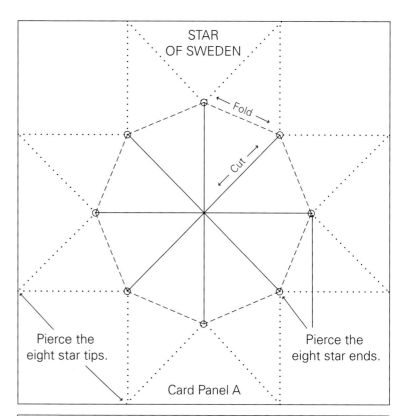

STAR
OF SWEDEN

Fold →

← Cut

Pierce the
eight star tips.

Pierce the
eight star ends.

Card Panel A

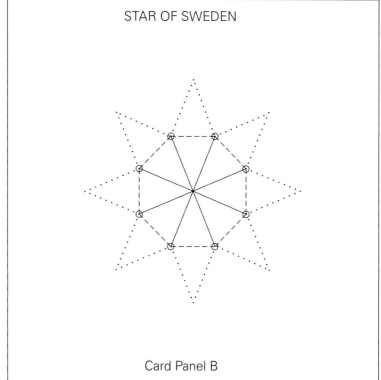

STAR OF SWEDEN

Card Panel B

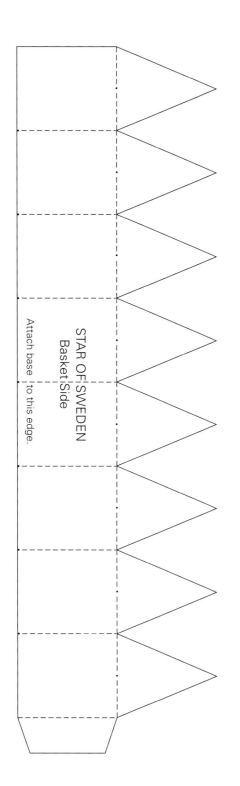

STAR OF SWEDEN
Basket Side

Attach base to this edge.

STAR OF SWEDEN

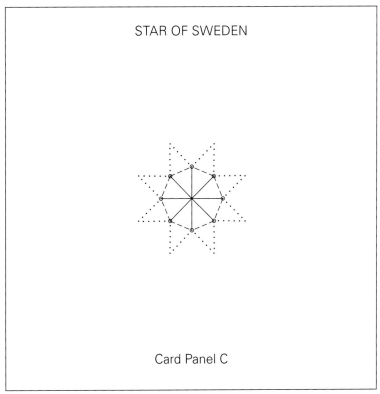

Card Panel C

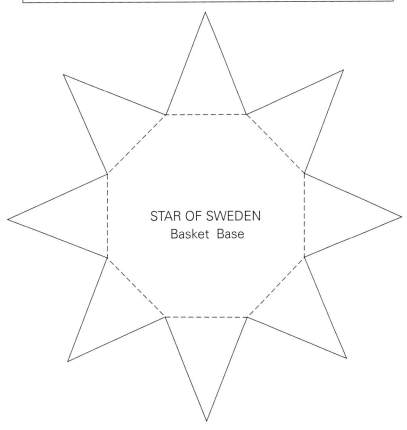

STAR OF SWEDEN
Basket Base

BLAZING SUN

Card

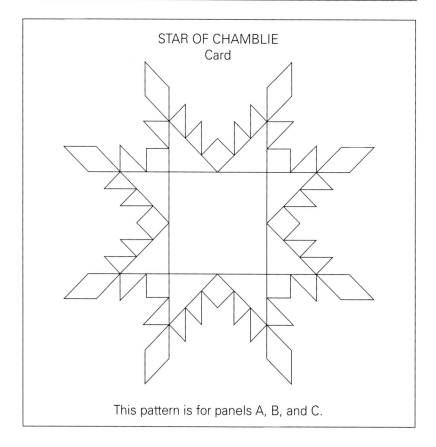

STAR OF CHAMBLIE
Card

This pattern is for panels A, B, and C.

TUMBLING BLOCKS
Card

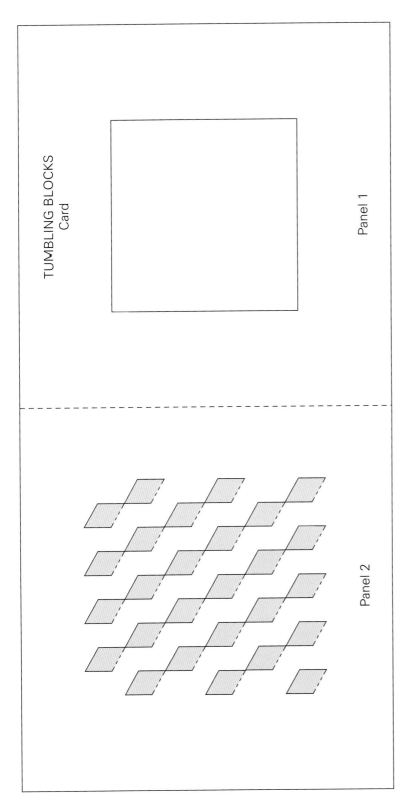

Panel 1

Panel 2

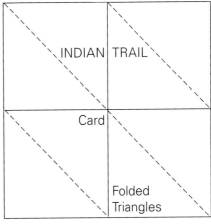

INDIAN TRAIL

Card

Folded
Triangles

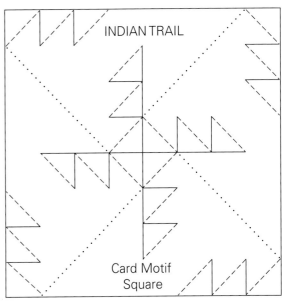

INDIAN TRAIL

Card Motif
Square

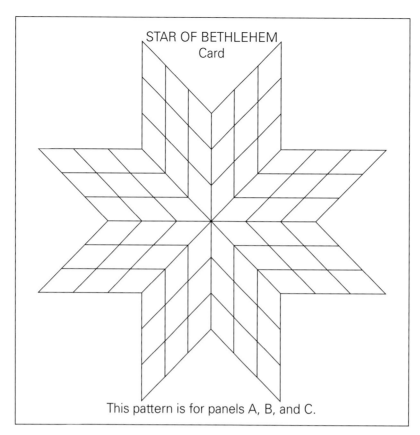

STAR OF BETHLEHEM
Card

This pattern is for panels A, B, and C.

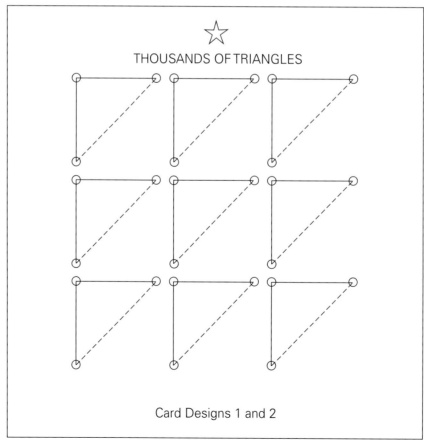

THOUSANDS OF TRIANGLES

Card Designs 1 and 2

WILD GOOSE	CHASE
.	.
	Card Design 1

WILD GOOSE	CHASE
.	.
	Card Design 1

.	.	.	.
.	WILD GOOSE CHASE .		.
.	.	.	.
.	Garland .	Pieces .	.

WILD GOOSE CHASE
Card Design 2
Center Star

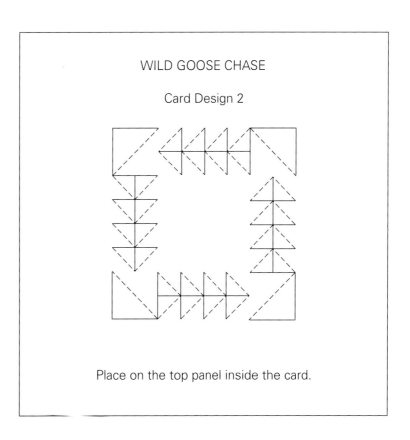

WILD GOOSE CHASE

Card Design 2

Place on the top panel inside the card.

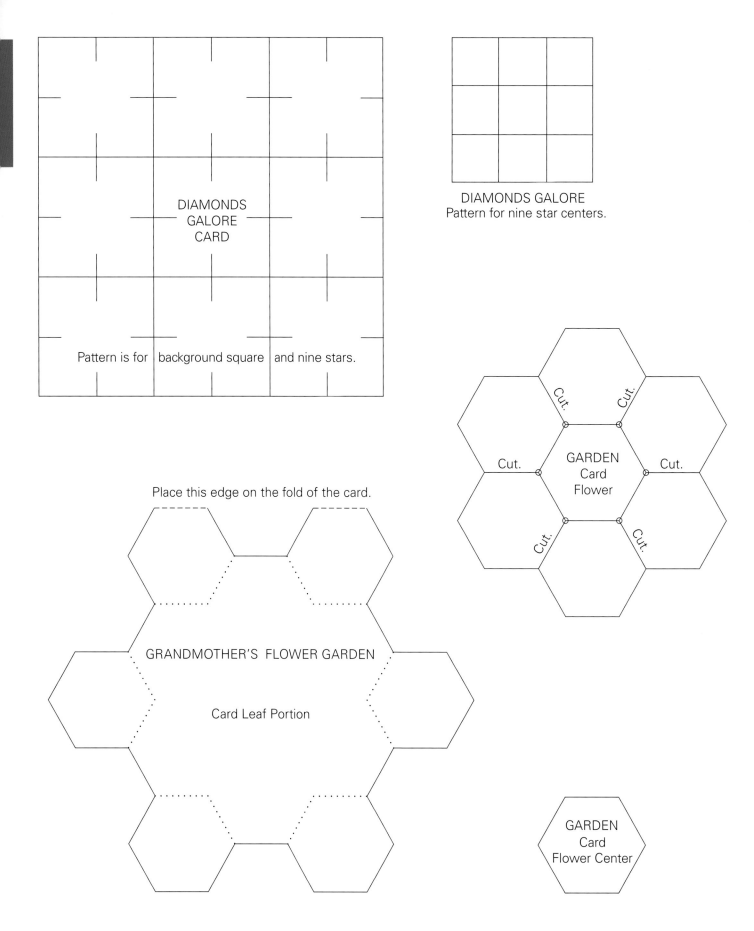

DIAMONDS
GALORE
CARD

Pattern is for | background square | and nine stars.

DIAMONDS GALORE
Pattern for nine star centers.

GARDEN
Card
Flower

Cut.   Cut.

Cut.   Cut.

Cut.   Cut.

Place this edge on the fold of the card.

GRANDMOTHER'S FLOWER GARDEN

Card Leaf Portion

GARDEN
Card
Flower Center

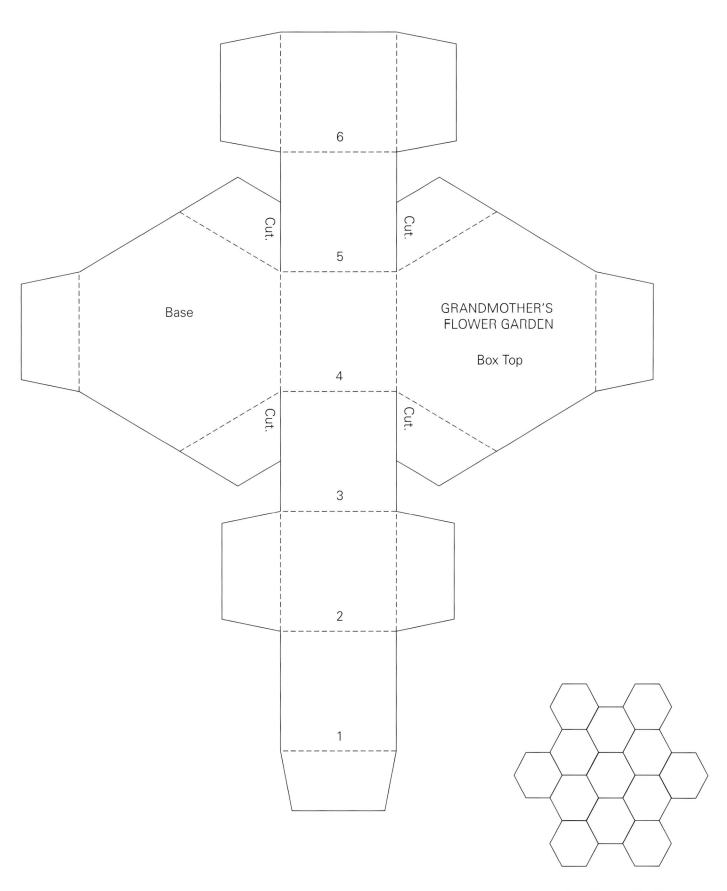

6

Cut.

Cut.

5

Base

GRANDMOTHER'S
FLOWER GARDEN

Box Top

4

Cut.

Cut.

3

2

1

Box Flower Motif

Place this edge on the fold of the card.

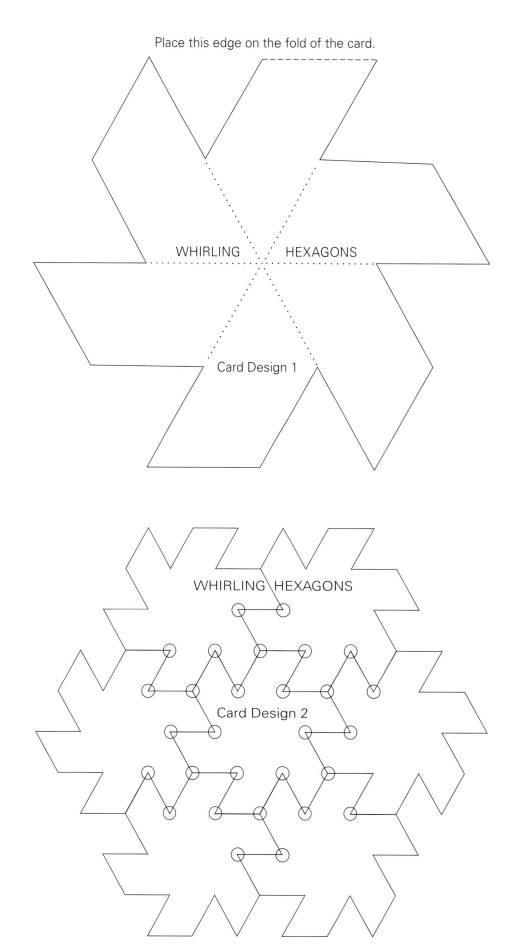

WHIRLING HEXAGONS

Card Design 1

WHIRLING HEXAGONS

Card Design 2

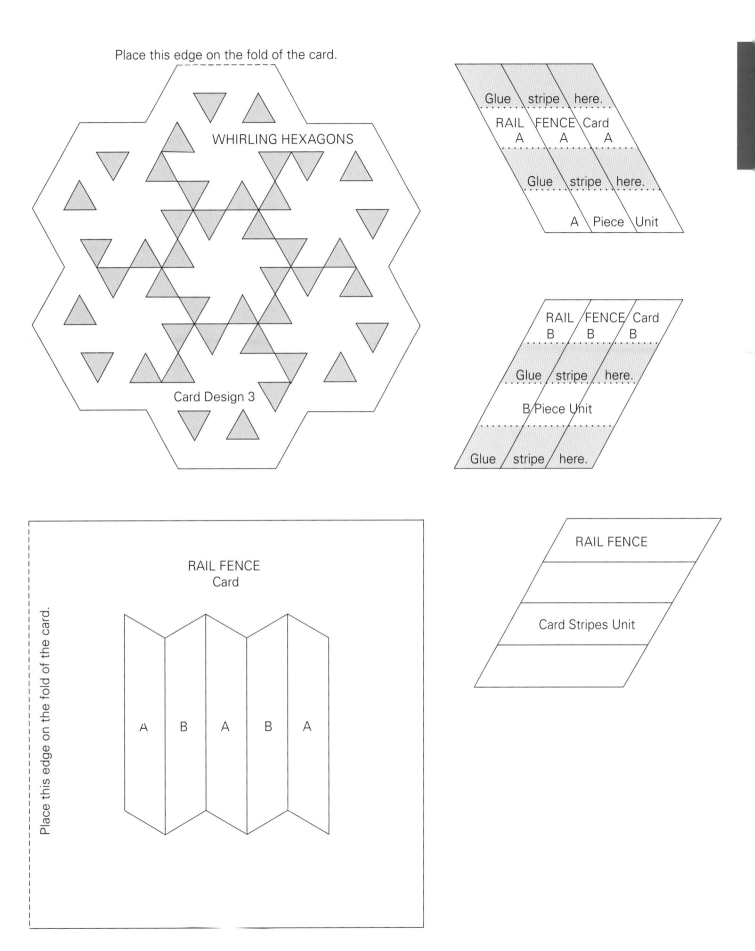

Place this edge on the fold of the card.

WHIRLING HEXAGONS

Card Design 3

Glue stripe here.

RAIL FENCE Card
A   A   A

Glue stripe here.

A   Piece   Unit

RAIL FENCE Card
B   B   B

Glue stripe here.

B Piece Unit

Glue stripe here.

Place this edge on the fold of the card.

RAIL FENCE
Card

A   B   A   B   A

RAIL FENCE

Card Stripes Unit

Place this edge on the fold of the card.

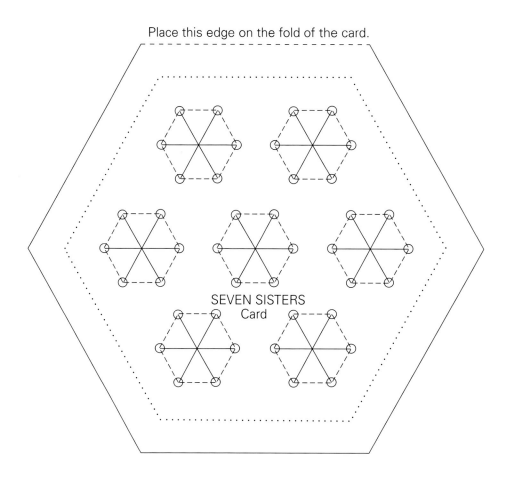

SEVEN SISTERS
Card

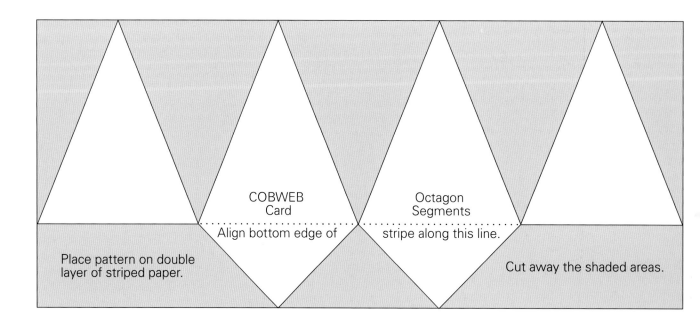

COBWEB
Card

Octagon
Segments

Align bottom edge of   stripe along this line.

Place pattern on double
layer of striped paper.

Cut away the shaded areas.

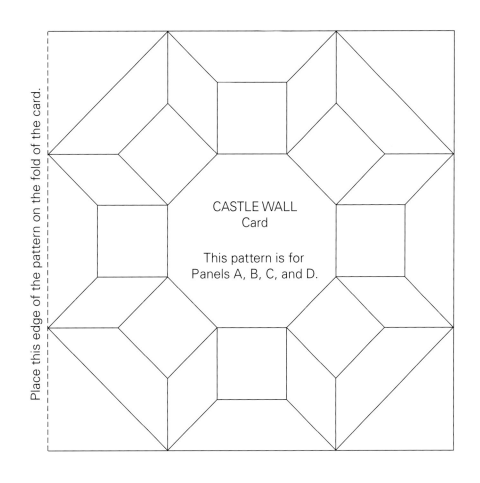

Place this edge of the pattern on the fold of the card.

CASTLE WALL
Card

This pattern is for
Panels A, B, C, and D.

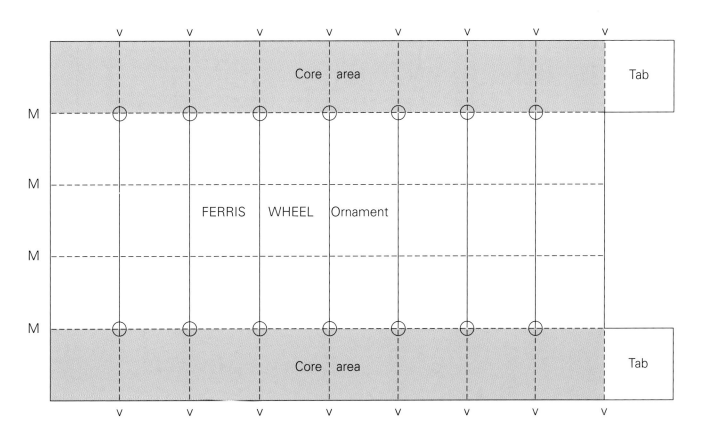

Core area

Tab

M

M

FERRIS   WHEEL   Ornament

M

M

Core area

Tab

INDEX

The pattern pages for the projects are in **bold**. Quilt motif names are CAPITALIZED.